WHAT EVERY VIR~~GINIA MILITARY WIFE~~
NEEDS TO KNOW ABOUT DIVORCE

A BOOK FOR MILITARY WIVES
AND FEMALE SERVICEMEMBERS

Matthew R. Hamel, Esq.
and
Charles R. Hofheimer, Esq.

www.VirginiaDivorceAttorney.com

In honor of women who serve
this country in invaluable, countless,
and often unsung ways.

Disclaimer
This book offers general information, not case-specific legal advice.
Please use this book for informational purposes only.

INTRODUCTION

Chances are, if you're reading this book, you are hurting and in the process of making a very important life decision. You are not happy in your marriage or with how this realm of your life has evolved. You are also married to the military or serving on active duty. In either case, we (Matt Hamel and Charlie Hofheimer) want to thank you for your service to our country. We want to acknowledge your service whether or not it was you or your spouse who signed up for the military. In the latter case, we know that all too often you shoulder the burdens and make the greatest sacrifices throughout your spouse's military career.

I (Matt Hamel, one of the co-authors of this book) have seen firsthand what military spouses confront watching my own wife cope as best she could. I know what it feels like to be helpless and half a world away and hear about a particularly difficult experience my spouse endured. I recall receiving an email from my wife while deployed to Iraq and learning of an incident the night before. My wife dragged three small children to the Portsmouth Naval Hospital emergency room despite the fact that only one needed to be there. I remember feeling helpless and completely unable to help her in a situation like that. Of course, under normal circumstances, one of us would have remained home with the other two children. In our case, she had a very good support network. However, she didn't want to burden any of her friends in the middle of the night and took on this entire responsibility herself. Even though I say "I get it," it is really only the military spouse who "gets it," and this is just one small example of the challenges military spouses confront every day. Military life, while often exhilarating and rewarding, can also be

3

extremely taxing and difficult on spouses and children, for whom there are no medals or other accolades.

So we want to thank you for the many change of station moves you've endured over the course of your, or your spouse's, military career – and even possibly the geo-bachelor tours you've endured. We always smile when our non-military friends remark how great it is to have the military pay for each and every move. What they don't understand are the literally hundreds of hidden costs that each move requires. Buying shower rods, toilet roll dispensers, soap dispensers, curtains, electric socket covers, among hundreds of other items, adds up. AND, all of this pales in comparison to the sacrifices you and your children make with these moves: new bedrooms, new neighbors and neighborhoods, different schools, new friends. A myriad of difficult obstacles arises with each relocation, and over time, this constant relocation can chip away at a family's sense of cohesion and rootedness. Each family member faces challenges, often at difficult and fragile intervals.

If you are reading this book, we understand that you are in the early stages of making a very meaningful life decision. We want you to know that you are educating yourself right now to help ensure you and your children have optimal success in your divorce proceedings. We have three simple goals for this book. First, we want you to not only be empowered with knowledge of the divorce process for the state of Virginia but also with entitlements that are unique to military divorces. Second, we want to help you make the best strategic family decisions for your life. We want to markedly reduce the fear of the unknown as you embark upon your decision making. In fact, we want you to take EVERYTHING OUT of the calculus of this equation EXCEPT what's best for YOU and YOUR CHILDREN. Third, we want to dramatically reduce your stress level. We can practically guarantee you that after reading this book you will know far more about military divorce in Virginia than most anyone, including your spouse.

We'd like you to use this book as your own personal *Sputnik* moment. By that we mean we want you to think about your life ten years down the line and picture where you want to be. If you absorb the guidance in this book, you will set yourself up in the best way possible for a divorce that supports you and your children's desires and goals. This entire experience will one day be far away in your rearview mirror. What you're doing here today is taking the first step towards protecting, educating, and empowering yourself... so that, in short order, you will be able to focus on where you want your life to be in ten years – and you will have the tools you need to arrive there successfully.

TABLE OF CONTENTS

PART IV–RESOURCES

WARNING AND DISCLAIMER

This book is in the nature of general information,
not specific legal advice.

Please use this book for informational purposes only.

WHO ARE THE AUTHORS OF THIS BOOK, AND WHY SHOULD I LISTEN TO THEM?

We believe you are here for a reason, and it's not just accidental or serendipitous that you came upon this book. If you believe in fate, then maybe you're here because of that. It doesn't necessarily mean you're about to have an epiphany. It simply means you are doing the necessary research and homework to best prepare yourself to make a very significant decision - and that you are here for a reason - particularly at this point in your decision-making process.

This reminds of us of the warning you receive on an airplane before take-off: "Make sure you put your own oxygen mask on first before helping your children or others." Quite simply, you need to take care of yourself first - emotionally, physically, and financially - because much is at stake for your and your children's present and future. Even the simplest divorce can be emotionally taxing. For some, it can also be traumatic. Once you read this book, you will be well positioned to shield yourself and your children from unnecessary stress and you will be informed about your rights and entitlements and how to protect them.

Matt Hamel and Charlie Hofheimer, Virginia divorce attorneys, are the co-authors of this book. Before joining the law firm of Hofheimer/Ferrebee, P.C., Matt served six years on active duty as a Navy JAG attorney. Hofheimer/Ferrebee represents women only in divorce. Three family members and one family friend founded the firm: Charlie, an attorney; his wife and paralegal, Diane Hofheimer; their daughter, attorney Kristen Hofheimer; and attorney Jack Ferrebee (Jack has since retired). They sensed a need to create a compassionate community of professionals to educate and represent women navigating through the divorce process. They wanted to provide Virginia women confronting divorce with resources, support, and advocacy. Today, Hofheimer/Ferrebee is an eight-lawyer Family Law firm dedicated exclusively to representing women in divorce and custody matters. Because so many military members live in the area, the firm has developed a strong arsenal of resources to specifically assist and support female military members and wives needing Family Law attorneys with keen understanding of the military and the unique situations women such as yourself are put in. Representing you means a great deal to us personally and professionally, and we understand that your quality of life and your children's is at stake. So, let's move forward.

1 THE DIVORCE PROCESS

Can a Military Jag Officer Represent Me in My Divorce?

Women frequently ask why a military attorney cannot represent one or both of the spouses in a divorce case. In the Navy, as well as in the other branches of the military, servicemembers are appointed free legal counsel to resolve various legal disputes. Divorce isn't one of them. For example, a servicemember or dependent wishing to notarize documents, execute a will, or create various powers of attorney has access to this counsel. However, when it comes to divorce, the process occurs in the state courts, and state law governs jurisdiction, child custody, child and spousal support, and property distribution.

As a prerequisite to becoming a JAG attorney or military attorney in any of the services, the lawyer must be licensed to practice law in one of the 50 states. Oftentimes a military attorney is licensed in a state other than the one in which he or she is stationed. Thus, the attorney, not licensed in the state in which he or she is stationed, cannot go into the civilian courts to represent the military servicemember. Also, as a policy, the military does not expect the taxpayers to help fund legal actions beyond a certain limited domain. Divorce and child custody case representation, while obviously extremely important, do not fall under the umbrella of JAG or military attorney services.

With that said, it is important to note that a servicemember or servicemember's spouse can visit a local legal service office at one of the military installations and seek free general advice about the divorce process. Many of these base legal offices have free resources and information about divorce in a particular area of that state, and there are attorneys in Legal Assistance offices often willing to provide general advice about the process. Such resources can be helpful and are worth checking out.

Initiating the Divorce Process

Most military wives and female service members who have made the decision to file a divorce hire a civilian attorney, and that person files what is known as a Complaint for Divorce (see page 17 for a sample Complaint). A Complaint contains facts like the date of marriage, date of separation, names of the children, birth dates of the children, location of the marriage, the parties' current residence and each party's location at the time of the separation. The Complaint also states each party's military status, grounds for divorce, or fault or no fault divorce status. This Complaint is then filed in the Circuit Court for the city where the divorcing couple last lived as a husband and wife or, alternatively, where the defendant currently resides This is generally how the process is initiated.

Service of Process

The actual divorce does not really start until your husband is served with the Complaint. This is known as "service of process." In Virginia, there are several ways in which service of process can be made on defendants. Personal service is when the complaint that you have filed is "physically" served to your husband. This can be done in many different ways; however, we generally prefer to hire private process servers. This way, we have more control over making sure where this occurs and that your husband is served in a timely manner.

Once your husband is served with the Complaint, within 21 days he is required to file an answer and he may choose to file a Counterclaim. In his response, he may deny many of the allegations against him, and his Counterclaim will likely assert certain allegations against you. It is not uncommon for his Counterclaim to have exaggerated allegations against you. Many times, this is designed to disturb or intimidate you. It's important to understand that if your case is actually litigated, he has to prove what he alleged, and if his allegations are untrue, he will look foolish and his credibility will diminish. So take a deep breath and know that words only have power over you if you allow them to have power. Stay calm, breathe deeply, and don't let him know you are upset. This will drive him crazy!

With military servicemembers, there is another added wrinkle with the service of process. Oftentimes the military servicemember is stationed outside the Commonwealth of Virginia and maybe even outside the United States. And sometimes, your spouse will try to avoid receiving the service of process. Thus, sometimes serving the Complaint can become a temporary problem, but, with a skilled attorney, it will be solved.

Residence and Domicile

It's important to be aware of the residence and domicile requirements of initiating a divorce action in Virginia. At the time the divorce suit is filed, either you or your husband must be and must have been an actual bona fide resident and domiciliary of Virginia for at least the preceding six months. The facts supporting the residence and domicile must be supported in your divorce Complaint. The residence and domicile requirements are two separate requirements, both of which must be proven in order for the court to have jurisdiction over your divorce action.

"Domicile" simply means that you or your husband live in a place permanently or at least indefinitely. Upon your separation, you may establish your own separate domicile. There are special rules governing residence and domicile of members of the armed forces. The governing statute provides the following: If a member of the armed forces of the United States has been stationed or has resided in Virginia for a period of six months or more immediately preceding the commencement of the divorce suit, then that person is presumed to be domiciled in and to have been a bona fide resident of Virginia. Your attorney can clarify this further should you have any specific questions on domicile status.

Service of Process

Returning to the service of process issue, this is really only an issue when the servicemember spouse chooses to be difficult. The majority of cases are handled and accomplished with few or no problems.

If the servicemember spouse is overseas and is willing to accept service by mail and/or waive future service, and then he signs and returns the documents, any service of process issue is resolved. Where this can become troublesome, however, is when the military servicemember remains on base in a foreign jurisdiction and voluntarily hides under military control. Military policy does not require the military member to accept process on the military installation. When a party wants to serve state court process on a servicemember in an area under military control, the amount of military assistance depends on the type of federal jurisdiction applicable in that area. Oftentimes the military authorities give the servicemember an opportunity to obtain legal advice and to refuse to accept the service. Then, the military authorities will simply return your notice to you, explaining that your husband has refused service of process. However, just because your husband is stationed at or maybe even living onboard a military installation does not mean you cannot ultimately accomplish serving your husband. It just may take longer than anticipated.

In fairly rare instances, the service of process can become very complicated, and some military authorities are easier to work with than others. Again, this is only an issue if the servicemember remains on base and outside the reach of our private process server or the local Sheriff's department. In most cases, military authorities on base will make the servicemember available for service of process. Most military installations have memorandums of understanding with the local county Sheriff's department. Essentially, what these agreements state is that the Sheriff will notify the military process officer that he desires to serve process on the service-member. The civil process officer, who normally works for the staff judge advocate on the base, will contact the service-member's command, and the command is responsible for ensuring that the servicemember is present at the base legal office on a designated day and time.

If your servicemember (husband) is stationed outside of Virginia, the process normally begins with your process server contacting the local Sheriff in that jurisdiction. The Sheriff will then advise the civil process officer on that base, and the military member will be given the opportunity to receive the service of process.

Again, the majority of service-of-process cases are handled without incident, and the process server is able to accomplish service successfully. In very rare circumstances (such as if your husband is stationed in a foreign country), international process servers can be used, and it is important for your attorney to research the local jurisdictional laws of that country in order to have your husband served properly.

One last point on service of process, if your husband has a girlfriend, we will often serve him when he is with her to let him know that **we know**. Sometimes when we serve your husband, we will also serve "her" with a notice of deposition so she can pressure him to get the case settled. Girlfriends do not want to go to court and be exposed for their adulterous behavior nor do they want to be cross-examined about the intimate details of their physical relationship with your husband. Serving him in this way often speeds up the divorce process.

SAMPLE COMPLAINT

1 VIRGINIA: IN THE CIRCUIT COURT OF THE CITY
OF VIRGINIA BEACH

JOAN A. SMITH,

        Plaintiff,

v.   CASE NO.: _____

WILLIAM R. SMITH,

        Defendant.

<u>COMPLAINT</u>

COMES NOW the Plaintiff, Joan A. Smith, by counsel, and for her complaint against the Defendant (Husband), states as follows to-wit:

1.   The parties are husband and wife having been lawfully married on June 20, 1995, in Virginia Beach, Virginia.

2.   There were two children born of the marriage, namely Rebecca L. Smith, born October 30, 1997, and Jason W. Smith, born April 19, 1999; there were no children born to either party and adopted by the other, nor adopted by the parties.

3.   The Plaintiff (Wife) is a resident and bona fide domiciliary of the Commonwealth of Virginia and has been for at least six months next preceding the filing of the suit for divorce.

4.   The Plaintiff (Wife) resides in the City of Virginia Beach and the Defendant (Husband) resides in the City of Virginia Beach.

5.   The parties last resided as husband and wife at 1245 Wolf Street in the City of Virginia Beach, Virginia.

6.   The Defendant (Husband) is a member of the Armed Forces of the United States.

7.   Both parties are of sound mind, over the age of 18 years, sui juris and neither party is incarcerated in a mental or penal institution.

8. On January 10, 2010, without just cause or provocation, the Defendant (Husband) deserted the Plaintiff (Wife) and the parties have been living separate and apart, uninterrupted and without marital cohabitation since that date and there is no likelihood of reconciliation.

9. That since the separation of the parties, the Defendant (Husband) has continuously bothered, molested and harassed your Plaintiff (Wife) to the extent that your Plaintiff (Wife)'s and the children's health and well-being are being impaired.

10. That the Defendant (Husband) has been guilty of cruelty toward the Plaintiff (Wife), causing reasonable apprehension of bodily harm in that the Defendant (Husband), over a period of many months physically abused, threatened, humiliated and degraded the Plaintiff (Wife) and subjected her to his violent and uncontrolled fits of temper, terrorizing the household; Defendant (Husband)'s conduct has completely deposed the Plaintiff (Wife) as a wife, rendered the marital state intolerable. Specifically on December 30, 2009, Defendant (Husband) pushed Plaintiff (Wife) up against a wall causing her to fall and on January 10, 2010 Defendant (Husband) threw a set of keys at Plaintiff (Wife) which struck her in her left arm leaving a bruise. Said conduct upon the part of the Defendant (Husband) is tantamount to constructive desertion, and the parties have been separated continuously since that time without interruption and without cohabitation and there is no likelihood of reconciliation.

11. That on diverse dates and locations including, but not limited to, December 29, 2009 and January 10, 2010 in Virginia Beach, Virginia, Defendant (Husband) has been guilty of adultery and/or sodomy with a person not your Plaintiff (Wife), whose name is Elaine B. Rushing, said adultery having taken place at the Notel Hotel located on Paramour Lane in Virginia Beach, Virginia. This adultery and/or sodomy has taken place within the past five years without the knowledge, consent or connivance of your Plaintiff (Wife), and the parties have lived separate and apart since January 10th, 2010 and that there is no likelihood of reconciliation.

WHEREFORE, and for as much as your Plaintiff (Wife) is remediless, save in a Court of Equity, your Plaintiff (Wife) prays that the said Defendant (Husband) be made a party to these proceedings; that all proper process may be issued; that a divorce, <u>A MENSA ET THORO</u>, pursuant to §20-95 of the Code of Virginia, 1950, as amended, be decreed your Plaintiff (Wife), to be later merged into a divorce <u>A VINCULO MAT-RIMONII</u> at the expiration of one year's separation on the grounds of desertion and cruelty pursuant to § 20-91(6) and adultery pursuant to §20-91(1) of the Code of Virginia, 1950, as amended; or, in the alternative, that a divorce <u>A VINCULO MATRIMONII</u> be decreed your Plaintiff (Wife) on the grounds of a one year separation pursuant to § 20-91(A)(9) (a) of the Code of Virginia, 1950, as amended; that the Plaintiff (Wife) be awarded attorney fees pursuant to § 20-103 to go forward with the suit both temporary and permanent, and Court costs; that the Plaintiff (Wife) be awarded custody of the children born of the marriage of the parties; that the Plaintiff (Wife) be awarded support money for the support, maintenance and education of said children; that the Plaintiff (Wife) be awarded temporary and permanent spousal support or a reservation of right; that the Defendant (Husband) be denied spousal support; that the Defendant (Husband) be required to maintain health and major medical insurance on the Plaintiff (Wife) and children; the Plaintiff (Wife) seeks an injunction against the Defendant (Husband) from bothering and harassing and otherwise interfering with the Plaintiff (Wife); that the Defendant (Husband) be restrained from contacting the Plaintiff (Wife) at home or at work, and from coming onto the premises where the Plaintiff (Wife) lives or works; that the Defendant (Husband) be restrained from discussing the divorce around the children of the marriage, and that he have no unrelated overnight guests of the opposite sex when the children have overnight visitation with him; the Plaintiff (Wife) seeks "equitable distribution" of the "marital property", monetary award, civilian or military retainer, and any other retirement pension, if any, pursuant to § 20-107.3 of the Code of Virginia and allocation of marital debt; for an injunction against the Defendant (Husband) requiring that he preserve his estate so that it will be forthcoming to meet any Decree which may be made in this suit, including an injunction enjoining and restraining him from disposing of any property, marital or otherwise, without court order; that the Plaintiff (Wife) be awarded exclusive use and possession of the marital residence so that she may reside there with the children; and that the Plaintiff (Wife) have such further and other relief in the premises as the nature of her cause may require or the Court in equity may deem meet and proper.

_____

Joan A. Smith

STATE OF VIRGINIA
CITY OF VIRGINIA BEACH, to-wit:

Before me, the undersigned Notary Public in and for the aforesaid City and State, personally appeared Joan A. Smith, who, after first being placed under oath, swore that the allegations contained in the foregoing Complaint are true to the best of her knowledge this _____ day of _____, 2011.

_____

Notary Public

My commission expires:_____

_____

Of Counsel

Charles R. Hofheimer, Esquire
Matthew R. Hamel, Esquire
HOFHEIMER/FERREBEE, P.C.
Sandpiper Key
1060 Laskin Road, Suite 12B
Virginia Beach, Virginia 23451
[757] 425-5200 phone [757] 425-6100 fax

Grounds for Divorce

We are routinely asked if Virginia is a No Fault Divorce state and what constitutes grounds for divorce here. The answer is extremely important because it is exactly what legitimates your divorce in a court of law.

The grounds for divorce are as follows:

a. A Separation of 6 months, if the parties have no minor children AND have entered into a Separation Agreement (no-fault);
b. A Separation of 12 months (no-fault);
c. Adultery, Sodomy, or Buggery;
d. Felony Conviction and Confinement;
e. Cruelty, or causing reasonable apprehension of bodily hurt," after a period of 1 year from the date of the acts; and
f. Willful desertion or abandonment, after a period of 1 year from the date of the act.

Adultery, Sodomy, Buggery

Many of our clients initially believe that the fault-based ground of adultery is an easy ground to assert. However, the reality is, adultery, as are sodomy and buggery, is difficult to prove in Virginia. Not only that, adultery cases are usually fraught with emotion and, oftentimes, unreasonable demands on both sides. A case involving a cheating spouse naturally heightens tension in a divorce case. It is important to set realistic goals with your attorney, develop a strategic litigation plan, and, above everything else, stick to the plan.

As stated, the fault grounds based on sexual misconduct are adultery, sodomy, and buggery. Adultery refers to any married person voluntarily having sexual intercourse with any person who is not his or her spouse. Sodomy grounds take place when any married person voluntarily engages in oral or anal sex with someone who is not his or her spouse, and buggery refers to sex with animals. While other grounds for divorce may be proven by a mere preponderance of the evidence (a more-likely-than-not standard), these sexual misconduct grounds require clear and convincing evidence. The proof must be clear, satisfactory, and conclusive in the eyes of the court. As with all divorce grounds, testimony or admissions must be corroborated. This means that the proof in front of the court must be some definitive evidence beyond mere suspicions or admissions by your husband that he had an affair. Specific evidence supporting allegations is particularly important in law suits brought on the ground of adultery.

So, how do you go about proving adultery (or sodomy or buggery) in a Virginia court? The easiest way is if your husband and his girlfriend have since broken up and she is willing to testify against him. If this girlfriend is willing to speak with your attorney, you may be able to put together several important facts about their relationship to help prove your case and even show that your husband is lying in court. For example, you and your attorney can learn how your husband and the girlfriend met, the locations of where they would often meet (a specific motel), and the dates and times of day that they got together. Of course, if the ex-girlfriend agrees to testify, it is easier to make your case.

To prove adultery, you must prove a sexual relationship; i.e., that your husband engaged in sexual intercourse with this other person. So how do you do this without the help of the girlfriend? Remember, a Hallmark card from another woman saying "I love you", or "Can't wait to see you again and be with you", or a text message saying, "I miss you", is not enough to prove adultery legally. You may know that an affair is taking or has taken place, yet proving this requires certain types of evidence. Your attorney will advise you as to how to best make this clear.

Maybe you have hired or are considering hiring a private investigator to help prove adultery has or is taking place. Some individuals may be good investigators but lousy in court under cross-examination. You need an investigator who is good at both. Again, your attorney can offer guidance here.

A good private investigator will compile the evidence necessary for you to prove the adultery in court. Even if you are lucky enough to document public displays of affection, such as walking hand-in-hand or perhaps kissing at a restaurant dinner table, that is still not enough evidence to prove Adultery. If, on the other hand, your investigator follows your husband and his girlfriend back to her house, videotapes them entering the home and his car remaining overnight or him leaving in the morning, you will come closer to meeting the "clear and convincing" burden of proof.

It is extremely important to remember that a court may not find that an adulterous relationship exists (beyond the legal burden of clear and convincing evidence), despite the obvious facts and evidence you have presented. This can be extremely unpleasant. We want you to know that there are many times one of our clients will allege adultery and tell us the specifics of her case. More often than not, we sympathize with this and believe her story to be true. Nevertheless, there are many instances where we simply do not believe we will be able to prove the adultery in court, at least not beyond the clear and convincing standard. This is not to say that we don't believe our client's story. It simply means that we need to be honest about the legal expectations and potentially adjust our litigation strategy. This doesn't mean we can't still allege and try to prove the adultery…it means we may need to look at other possible grounds for divorce as well and be prepared to wait the jurisdictional 1-year waiting period.

IMPORTANT WARNINGS

As we progress, we have a few very important warnings for you from a legal standpoint. Please take the following guidance to heart so as not to weaken your case.

1. **DO NOT SLEEP WITH YOUR HUSBAND**. If your husband has had an affair, and you engage in sex with him after learning of the marital infidelity, you have just condoned the adultery in the eyes of the law. This concept is known as **condonation.** Condonation occurs when the injured party knows of the marital offense and freely consents to the restoration of marital rights. This means that the ground of adultery is no longer available to you as a fault-based ground for divorce and you are required to wait the minimum 12-month separation period. The sexual acts of adultery, sodomy, and buggery are the only grounds in Virginia that do not require the waiting period of 1 year before you can get divorced. Therefore, if you can prove one of these has occurred, you can get divorced.

2. The court may deny a divorce based on evidence of **connivance.** Connivance occurs when one spouse sets the other one up for a fault ground.

3. If a spouse is guilty of adultery or sodomy and it is proved sufficiently in a Virginia court, then the court **shall not award permanent** maintenance or spousal support to the guilty spouse (there is a very narrow exception to this rule). It is important to note that there is a five-year statute of limitation on adultery - so an affair that occurred more than five years ago should be of no legal consequence. Further, if you have committed adultery,

24

never admit it to anyone unless and until you talk to your lawyer. And, you should talk to an attorney immediately.

4. There is also a concept in Virginia law called **manifest injustice.** If the court determines by clear and convincing evidence that a denial of support or maintenance would constitute a manifest injustice, based on the respective degrees of fault during the marriage and the relative economic circumstances of the parties, the court can nonetheless make a spousal support award to the spouse committing Adultery. Note, this is a very difficult argument to make to the court. It is a last-ditch effort where special circumstances exist.

Felony Conviction and Confinement

A few more important items deserve mentioning. A divorce due to a felony conviction is possible if your husband is indeed convicted of a felony, sentenced to confinement for more than 1 year, and confined following the court's decree. The person filing for divorce due to a felony conviction must not cohabit with his or her spouse after learning of the confinement or this ground is no longer feasible.

Cruelty

A divorce may be granted based upon cruelty or reasonable apprehension of bodily hurt after 1 year has elapsed since the acts complained of. Acts of physical violence and conduct that endanger the life, safety, or health of the plaintiff constitute cruelty. Abusive language, humiliating statements, and repeated neglect can also constitute cruelty. While cruelty is often shown by a succession of acts, a single act of cruelty is sufficient if it is a very serious act. Where a spouse drinks alcohol to excess, cruelty is not shown unless it is coupled with other acts that constitute misconduct.

The courts will distinguish between normal conduct of unhappy people and cruel conduct on the part of one of the spouses. Because of the available option to the court to declare a no fault divorce based on a 1-year separation, many of our clients file on cruelty, but few divorces are actually ultimately granted on the grounds of cruelty. More often than not, the court or the parties will opt out for a 1 year separation no-fault divorce, either because they negotiated a Separation Agreement or because they don't want to spend the substantial money necessary to put on a fault ground divorce.

Willful Desertion or Abandonment

A divorce may be granted on the ground of willful Desertion or Abandonment after 1 year has elapsed since the alleged act. There must be proof of (i) the actual breaking off of the matrimonial cohabitation and (ii) an intent to desert in the mind of the offender. Both are required. Desertion does not occur when the husband and wife mutually consent to a separation.

Quite simply, desertion requires proof that a party has left the marital home with the intent not to return. This intent may be proven by actions, words, or conduct. We often advise our clients who need to leave the marital residence for a short period of time to write a note to their spouses saying something along the lines of "I am going to my mother's, but I shall return in two weeks." If you write such a note, keep a copy of it, as oftentimes your spouse will allege that he did not receive it. It is important that you actually return to the marital residence. Otherwise you could be found guilty of desertion.

Many of our clients have had occasions where the husband has left the marital home. Unfortunately, the husband then meets with an attorney and realizes he is guilty of desertion and moves back. If you have not filed for divorce before he returns, you are probably stuck with him in the home until you work out a settlement. This obviously puts great stress on the family, and yet, the courts are very reluctant to force anyone to leave home absent any family abuse. So, if your husband leaves, and you believe divorce is inevitable, our advice is that you file a Complaint for Divorce immediately.

Constructive Desertion

Constructive Desertion is a complex legal term referring to various ways a spouse may dishonor his marriage. Constructive Desertion may be found when a spouse refuses to engage in sexual intercourse, without justification, and other significant marital duties are not fulfilled. Constructive Desertion can also be present when the actions of your spouse are so adverse to the welfare of your family that you are, in essence, forced to leave the marital residence for your safety and well-being. However, we advise you to be cautious about alleging this ground for divorce without seeking legal advice as it, too, requires legally admissible "proof."

No Fault Divorce

A no fault divorce may be granted based upon a separation of 6 months if (i) the parties have entered into a separation agreement and (ii) there are no minor children. The separation must be one in which the husband and wife have lived separately and apart without any cohabitation and without interruption for the required period of time. Additionally, at least one of the parties must have intended for the separation to be permanent at the time the separation commenced.

If there are minor children, or if there is no written agreement, a final decree of divorce may also be granted based upon a separation of 12 months. As with the 6-month separation, the parties must have lived separately and apart without any cohabitation and without interruption for the full 12 months, and at least one of the parties must have intended for the separation to be permanent at the time it commenced.

A no fault divorce essentially eliminates the need to prove fault in order to obtain a divorce.

Fault Versus No Fault – Does it Matter Which One?

You may be wondering if it matters whether or not you file a no fault divorce case. It does matter - and it can matter a great deal. If you file a fault-based divorce, then, in many jurisdictions, you can get into court within three or four weeks. In order to file a no fault divorce, you must have been separated for 6 months (if you have a signed agreement and no minor children), or for 1 year without an agreement. This can matter quite a bit if you do not have adequate finances while waiting to get into court.

It is also very important to note that with a no fault divorce, you can only file for custody, visitation, child support, and spousal support in the Juvenile and Domestic Relations District Court. This court is lower than the Circuit Court (the one that later will grant your final divorce). If you do file in the Juvenile and Domestic Relations District Court for custody and support, your husband can file an appeal which will entail more legal expenses and more waiting. If your husband is ordered to pay you support in the Juvenile and Domestic Relations Court, he will have to pay you that support while awaiting his appeal. However, be cautious…your husband could choose to file a divorce case the day before your Juvenile and Domestic Relations Court hearing (for the custody, child support/spousal support), further delaying your ability to obtain custody and support. Make sure you discuss all of this with your attorney when planning your litigation strategy.

If you decide to file a fault-based divorce, then you file in the Circuit Court, and you can also file for what is called *pendente* lite relief. Unlike the hearing in Juvenile and Domestic Relations Court, at a pendente lite hearing, a Circuit Court judge can order exclusive possession of the residence to one of the parties as well as certain other forms of relief. This means, that in addition to being admitted into Circuit Court more quickly, the court can provide injunctions against your husband for squandering assets and other specific reckless actions. Again, with the fault grounds, you do not have a waiting period regarding the filing of the divorce, and normally it is easier to have your case heard without a long delay.

Filing for divorce on fault grounds can affect your divorce substantively if you are able to prove your grounds. Of course, you can expect additional legal expenses related to proving your grounds as well. Fault can affect spousal support, property distribution, and custody issues - but not necessarily guaranteed. You should discuss the potential costs and benefits of a fault-based divorce in your particular situation with your attorney.

Pendente Lite Relief

A pendente lite hearing permits you and your husband to ask for temporary help pending the outcome of your divorce (see page 31). If necessary, the court can temporarily order exclusive possession of the marital home to either you or your husband; custody and visitation regarding your minor children; child and spousal support; attorneys fees to carry on the suit; non-harassment conditions; and a limited number of additional orders regarding the marital assets and other issues. As of July 1, 2011, a Judge can also order joint and/or individual debts be paid by one party at a Pendite Lite hearing.

A temporary hearing is like putting a bandage on a gushing wound—the court is trying to sort out each of your needs while determining each of your abilities to pay. Add to the equation the reality that you and your husband now constitute two households instead on one and your problems become magnified, especially if there were financial problems before your divorce was filed.

SAMPLE NOTICE OF TEMPORARY RELIEF

1   VIRGINIA: IN THE CIRCUIT COURT OF THE CITY OF VIRGINIA BEACH

JOAN A. SMITH,

    Plaintiff,

v.   CASE NO.: _____

WILLIAM R. SMITH,

    Defendant.

N O T I C E

PLEASE TAKE NOTICE that on Friday, April 15, 2011 at 9:30 a.m., or as soon thereafter as counsel may be heard, the undersigned shall move this Honorable Court for entry of an order, pendente lite, awarding Plaintiff (Wife) custody of the child(ren) born of the marriage; support money for the support, maintenance and education of said child(ren); temporary and permanent spousal support for her support and maintenance;   medical and hospitalization coverage for the Plaintiff (Wife) and child(ren); attorney's fees and costs associated herewith; an Order enjoining the Defendant (Husband) from disposing of any personal or marital assets from the estate to ensure that they will be available to meet any decree which may be entered in this suit; an Order enjoining the Defendant (Husband) from bothering, harassing or otherwise interfering with the Plaintiff (Wife) and restraining him from contacting her at home or at work, and from coming onto the premises where the Plaintiff (Wife) lives or works; that Defendant (Husband) be restrained from discussing the divorce around the child(ren) of the marriage; that the Defendant (Husband) have no unrelated overnight guests of the opposite sex when the child(ren) have overnight visitation with him and that the child(ren) have absolutely no contact with Defendant (Husband)'s paramours; that the Plaintiff (Wife) be awarded exclusive use and possession of the marital residence so that she may reside there with the child(ren) ; that Plaintiff (Wife) be awarded attorney fees pursuant to § 20-103 to go forward with the suit both temporary and permanent, and Court costs; and for such further and other relief as in equity may seem meet or the nature of her cause deems just.

JOAN A. SMITH

By_____
                        Of Counsel

Charles R. Hofheimer, Esquire
Matthew R. Hamel,Esquire
HOFHEIMER/FERREBEE, P.C.
1060 Laskin Road, Suite 12B
Virginia Beach, VA 23451
(757) 425-5200
(757) 425-6100 fax

What Possible Defenses Could Your Husband Assert to Bar the Court from Granting Your Divorce on the Grounds You Are Seeking?

We want to mention at this point that there are several affirmative defenses that your husband could assert that could bar the court from granting you a divorce on the grounds you are seeking. Now that you know what your grounds for filing a divorce are, it is important to know what to expect from the other side. You will want to discuss this with your attorney as you plan your litigation strategy. A quick note about the term, litigation strategy: We use this term to discuss the strategy session you should have with your attorney when planning the overall blueprint of your case. It does not necessarily mean you will actually engage in active litigation in court. In fact, the vast majority of divorce cases settle - it is usually a matter of when the case settles in the process rather than if the case will settle. However, you should never fear litigation. If your attorney is afraid to litigate, that is a clear sign you should seek another attorney. While most cases do settle, we are always ready for those cases in which one party refuses to settle. We look forward to a case being litigated...and you should too...provided you have planned a sound litigation strategy with your attorney.

In general, the granting of a divorce on the requested grounds may be barred by a variety of procedural defects or doctrines. First, the court may lack jurisdiction to grant a divorce if neither party satisfies the residence and domicile requirements we referenced earlier. If the court lacks jurisdiction over the defendant (husband), it may not be permitted to grant certain forms of relief to you. And, even in cases where the court has jurisdiction over the action, a divorce may be barred if no valid marriage can be proven. If you were married in a foreign jurisdiction while stationed abroad, you will most certainly want to discuss this marriage ceremony with your attorney. As we also discussed before, a five-year statute of limitations may bar a divorce on the ground of Adultery. Finally, where a divorce has been granted, the judgment may be attacked based on alleged fraud.

We referred to **Condonation** earlier. Condonation occurs when the injured party knows of the marital offense and freely consents to the restoration of marital rights. This is usually evidenced by a resumption of cohabitation or sexual intercourse. Condonation should always be pled as an affirmative defense. However, even where condonation is not pled as a defense, the court may deny a divorce where the evidence shows that the plaintiff has condoned the marital fault complained of.

Also, even in divorce cases, be aware that the **insanity** defense can be pled. Most people think of this defense as applicable to a criminal trial, but it actually can be used in broader ways. In the case of divorce, in order for any party to be at fault, that party must have the mental capacity to understand the nature and repercussions of his or her actions. In fairly rare cases, this defense may surface, and your attorney can guide you through the legal workings and advise you about how to best proceed.

Recrimination is another affirmative defense and it refers to cases when both spouses are guilty of marital fault. This is usually best exemplified in a case where a wife learns of her husband's infidelity - and she then chooses to have an affair to exact revenge. In cases like this, the court will grant neither of the parties a divorce based on the ground of adultery.

The court may also deny a divorce based on evidence of **Connivance.** As noted, connivance occurs when one spouse knowingly consents to or sets up the misconduct of the other spouse, such as the couple participating in a threesome. Similarly, a wife cannot set her husband up with a prostitute and then file for divorce on Adultery grounds because her husband sleeps with the prostitute.

Lastly, a spouse charged with desertion can always answer with the defense of **Justification for Leaving.** Justification for Leaving may be raised whenever the misconduct of one spouse is so serious that it makes the relationship intolerable and the court concludes that the other spouse cannot reasonably be expected to remain in the marital home. This ground applies to extreme cases, and we can advise if this applies to your situation and direct our legal strategy accordingly.

The Separation Agreement

In most divorce cases, the separation agreement is a very important document. First and foremost, the separation agreement is often the result of lengthy negotiations, mediation, collaboration, and sometimes, litigation. Clearly, the majority of divorce cases conclude with a separation agreement. This may sound a bit odd since we only discussed the separation agreement as necessary in some of the no fault divorce cases. However, separation agreements are often the most important document in a divorce – and often are incorporated into the document that finalizes your divorce.

So what is the separation agreement and what specifically must it include? The separation agreement is a document in which you contractually agree upon a division of your marital property and other assets, terms of spousal and child support as well as child custody matters, pension and retirement allocations, insurance coverage, tax planning, and many other important issues arising from your marriage. It is also called a property settlement agreement. It is not an agreement to separate or a temporary agreement governing the terms of your separation until divorce or reconciliation. It is intended to be a final settlement of all issues between you and your husband. When you cannot agree on something – such as alimony or pension division – you must not simply leave it out. This is why it is extremely important for your attorney to review the terms of your separation agreement with you. The separation agreement governs most, if not all, of the conduct you and your spouse shall engage in while your divorce winds its way through the divorce process–and often thereafter, forevermore. Your attorney will advise you of how to handle contentious yet significant aspects of the agreement.

In this area, if you omit something that both parties can't agree on, it is waived. Many separation agreements contain a "general release clause," and if your husband is the primary wage earner in your family, you can bet that his attorney will put this clause in your agreement. This clause states that "any rights or claims not set out in the agreement are waived." Let's say you and your husband can't agree on how much alimony you should be paid and you believe you can litigate or resolve the issue later. If you have a "general release clause" and you also do not write, "The parties cannot agree on alimony; therefore this issue is reserved for later agreement between them or for a court decision on the matter," THEN YOU HAVE JUST WAIVED ALIMONY – and it may be lost under state law. At the very least, it will be expensive to re-litigate an issue or issues that could have been more constructively addressed.

This can be particularly important when dividing a military pension. It is common practice to agree on military pension division or property settlement in a separation agreement and then follow up with the Military Pension Division Order (topics that will be touched upon later). If you intend to include division of the pension AND survivor benefit plan coverage, then you ought to say so in the separation agreement. If you intend to leave one of these out, particularly if you are the female, active duty, servicemember – then you ought to clearly indicate this in the separation agreement as well. Remember, survivor benefit plan coverage is not division of the pension. The survivor benefit plan is an annuity that replaces the pension – particularly since the death of the servicemember terminates pension payments. If you have vague wording in your separation agreement regarding the pension, this will not preserve survivor benefit plan coverage. If your separation agreement simply states that you will receive one-half of the marital share of the military pension– you may be out of luck when it comes to the survivor benefit plan. A good attorney will not overlook this very important factor.

Since most divorce cases ultimately conclude with the separation agreement, it is imperative to properly negotiate the terms of the separation agreement and to take timing into account. **IT IS EXTREMELY IMPORTANT THAT YOU NEVER SIGN ANY DOCUMENT WITHOUT FIRST HAVING IT REVIEWED BY YOUR ATTORNEY.** If your husband asks you to sign something in return for a verbal concession of some sort, DO NOT SIGN THE DOCUMENT. We have seen many agreements signed by a wife that end up seriously reducing her entitlements. If you remember one piece of advice from this book, it should be: Think before signing any document that you have not had reviewed by your attorney. Many signed documents are binding and can hamper your rights permanently.

Benefits of a Written Separation Agreement

We can't stress to you enough the importance of a good, written separation agreement. Simply stated, your separation agreement is your <u>Bill of Rights</u>, your <u>Constitution</u> and your <u>Declaration of Independence</u> all rolled up in one document!

One of the major benefits of a mutually agreed upon separation agreement is that a court will almost always adopt the reasonable compromises you and your husband have agreed upon and will respect your decision about child custody. You and your husband are in the best position to understand what custody arrangement is best for your child. If you and your husband can agree on this, then this would remove a major obstacle that is often the subject of costly and lengthy litigation.

For example, with a signed separation agreement, you and your husband can be more creative and make stipulations beyond the court's normal jurisdiction. Although Virginia law generally holds that a parent does not have the duty to pay for his or her child's college education, such an obligation will be enforced if the parties agree to it in a separation agreement. If you can get your husband to agree to pay for college for the kids and he agrees to this in the separation agreement, it will be enforced even if he later changes his mind!

In Virginia, a trial court judge does not have the authority to order a divorced husband to contract for life insurance and name you as the beneficiary in a divorce decree…unless there is a preexisting policy. However, this can be done with the parties' consent in a Separation Agreement.

And very importantly…a Virginia trial judge cannot include a clause that later will "escalate" a support award in your divorce decree…particularly if it is premised on uncertain future circumstances. However, with a separation agreement, a carefully constructed "escalator clause" may be a valid provision.

Upon your divorce, your separation agreement will be incorporated into the divorce decree, and the court can have the same contempt powers over the enforcement of the separation agreement as it would have over any other divorce decree. This means that if your husband fails to perform his obligations under the separation agreement, he can be held in contempt of court - and you can utilize the court to actually enforce this Agreement.

If you and your husband do not contractually settle your support, custody and property rights prior to a divorce in a separation agreement, the only available alternative left may be litigation in court, which can be emotionally, physically AND financially costly.

The Discovery Process

Once a divorce has been filed, you need to arm yourself with all of the facts and make sure your attorney knows every detail about your marital home, estate and family situation. This process is the Discovery Process. So, how do you go about obtaining all of this information concerning your expenses, income, and investments, particularly if your husband is usually in charge of all of the finances? The easiest and most cost-effective way is to file Interrogatories. Interrogatories are comprised of a list of questions which ask details about assets, liabilities, fault, custody issues and arrangements, and anything else that may be relevant in your case. These questions can include information about income, bank accounts, retirement accounts, investments, hours worked, insurance policies owned, vacation and sick leave accrued, and other financial factors. These interrogatories can also be useful in identifying potential witnesses having knowledge about your particular case.

You can also request that your husband provide documents or other tangible items that are in his possession or accessible to him and which are relevant to your case.

Another method to discover information is to depose the other party. This can be a rather expensive way to go about getting all of the evidence in your case, but in a deposition, your husband is compelled to appear with his attorney in your attorney's office to answer questions under oath before a court reporter and you. Since these statements are then under oath, they may be later admitted as evidence in court. These depositions can also be taken of other people, such as your husband's girlfriend and your children's babysitters or teachers - who may have valuable information. Much of this information can be used as evidence in court, and certain details can prove highly advantageous to your case.

Another effective tool in the discovery process is what is called Request for Admissions. Admissions are admit or deny questions posed to your husband that must be answered within 21 days. A failure to answer the admissions will actually constitute an admission in court - and can be extremely useful. This is important - especially if you are served a request for admissions by your husband. Make sure that if Admissions are served to you that you thoroughly consult with your attorney before answering any admissions from your husband's attorney and that you answer in a timely fashion.

Finally, if your husband claims he has turned over everything, but you still believe he is lying, you can then file what is known as a "subpoena duces tecum." Normally this deals with financial information that your husband may be trying to hide. In this case, you will send a subpoena duces tecum to his employer requesting documents that will provide information about his income, benefits, retirement funds, and earned vacation time as well as copies of his last twelve month pay records. This can also help with other records kept by third parties that are relevant to your case.

It is important to note that obtaining each of the above costs money and time to obtain the information requested. As part of your litigation strategy, you will want to discuss what documents you already have in your possession and what documents you think you might be able to obtain on your own before employing some of the more costly discovery methods. However, at the end of the day, having more information than is necessary is always better than not enough. You do not want to settle your case only to learn later that there were significant assets or income which were available to you that you walked away from because you were not aware of their existence.

Alternative Dispute Resolution

Once you have received all of the relevant discovery information detailed above, you are now in a position to discuss with your attorney what method will be the most efficient and cost effective to successfully complete the divorce process. There are essentially four ways to accomplish this: 1) Negotiations leading to a successful separation agreement; 2) Mediation; 3) Collaboration; and 4) Litigation.

Negotiation leading to a Separation Agreement

We have already discussed how the vast majority of cases are settled through the use of separation agreements. However, we did not discuss the "negotiations" leading up to an agreed-upon separation agreement. It is not uncommon for one side to provide the other side with written offers of the terms under which he or she would agree to settle the divorce. Then the other side would respond with its' terms. A give-and-take process then unfolds until all of the issues are resolved. This can happen through correspondence between attorneys or in a settlement meeting with you, your attorney, your husband and his attorney. Once the parties agree on all of the family issues, the terms are then distilled into a separation agreement – and this document will then become the final terms of your divorce, and in many instances, will constitute your final decree of divorce.

Mediation

Mediation is potentially a cost effective alternative to litigation. However, be cautious. Divorce mediation is not feasible for all parties – and this process requires a mutual goal between the parties to settle all disputes in a non-adversarial manner. If you are intimidated by your husband or you do not feel that you have sufficient knowledge of your assets to make informed choices, make sure you discuss this with your attorney. Similarly, speak with your attorney before going into the mediation process to make sure you develop an outline of the issues and an acceptable range of terms on each issue that you would be willing to accept in an agreement.

So what exactly is divorce mediation? Divorce mediation is a process where the parties to a divorce are assisted by an impartial, professional mediator in reaching an agreement on the issues in the divorce. You will discuss issues such as child and spousal support, child custody, and division of the marital property. Remember that the mediator is not trying to "reconcile" you and your husband in the marriage. Rather, he or she is aiding you in procuring a divorce with a minimum of adversarial hostility and expense. The mediator may be an attorney – but he or she is not there to give you specific legal advice on what is best in your case or to make sure that any agreement reached is fair. It is your responsibility to be prepared to ask for what you want in mediation and to know where you are willing to compromise or when you should be prepared to walk away from mediation.

Collaboration

Collaborative law is a rather new form of alternative dispute resolution in Virginia. It differs from mediation in that it does not involve the use of a neutral third-party in the decision-making process. In the collaborative model, each side is represented by an attorney trained in collaborative law. The other members of the collaborative team may include a neutral child specialist, a neutral financial specialist and divorce coaches for you and your husband. Then, all parties, with the help of their collaborative team, engage in direct negotiations – in conference-like settings. These conferences are designed for the parties to engage in problem-solving and the team members from both sides can contribute creative ideas and assist in negotiating a settlement to all of the issues.

A few words of caution are in order here: first, the collaborative law model is premised on the fact that both sides will voluntarily disclose all relevant information. In addition, both parties and their attorneys sign a collaborative agreement and the attorneys CANNOT later represent either party in any subsequent related litigation against the other party.

This process is new and permits couples to work through issues involving their children, financial future and property distribution using problem-solving techniques without going to court. The attorneys work together with the team of coaches, child specialists, financial specialists and other professionals to reach an agreement that addresses all of the interests and priorities of both spouses – as well as the whole family. For more information about collaborative divorce, go to:

www.VirginiaCollaborativeLaw.com
or
www.collaborativepractice.com

Litigation

Another method is litigation, the most costly process for getting divorced. Litigation simply means fighting it out in court. Sometimes you are forced into litigating every issue in your case because your husband (or your husband's attorney) is being completely unreasonable. When this happens, you then have a trial presided over by a judge. There are no jury trials in Virginia divorce cases. In such cases, the judge will then make rulings (decisions) regarding each and every issue upon which you and your husband were unable to agree. The final divorce decree is then entered based upon the judge's decision.

When litigating any case, remember this: "failing to prepare is preparing to fail." You and your attorney need to be prepared for every circumstance that may come up in your case. You should not withhold any information from your attorney - no matter how awkward it might be to mention. Remember, your attorney is your advocate - and anything you say to him or her is protected via the Attorney-Client privilege. If your attorney is caught off guard in court with information you could have easily provided, then your case is handicapped.

If you anticipate that litigation will be your only option this still does not mean you cannot get your husband to agree to certain terms. It just means that the process will be protracted and that you and your attorney will need the time to become adequately prepared before you "do battle" in court.

What Happens after the Divorce Decree is Final?

After your trial, the attorney will draft a final decree of divorce based on the court's decision and it will be entered by the court. Should you believe you were granted an unfair judgment that is legally incorrect by the court in your divorce, you can appeal. You must, however, file this with the Court of Appeals within thirty days from the date of the court's final order. Ultimately and in rare circumstances, the Supreme Court of Virginia, at its discretion, can certify a case for review.

The appeal process in Virginia is expensive and it can take six months to a year or more to resolve. You should also know that the factual findings of the trial court will not be disturbed on appeal unless you can show that the order was plainly wrong and that it was not supported by a preponderance of the evidence. What this means is that it is very difficult – both procedurally and factually – to overturn your case from the trial level. You need to take your trial extremely seriously and consult with your attorney before filing any appeal.

2 CHILDREN & FINANCES

You now know about the general process of getting divorced in Virginia. As mentioned in the beginning, you will most likely know more about your divorce than your husband after reading this book. Believe it or not, you now also have a working vocabulary of many of the legal terms your attorney will use throughout your divorce case. To build upon what we have already covered, next we'll focus on strategy and then we'll cover some of the more intricate aspects of temporary relief, spousal support, child support, equitable distribution, retirements, and child custody.

If you are feeling a bit overwhelmed...don't worry. Your divorce case is complicated and you are not expected to fully comprehend each and every concept we discuss here in the book and how it applies to your case. Your attorney will help you understand what's important in your unique situation and guide you through the process now that you have a basic familiarity with what to expect. Your divorce case can involve motions, litigation, complex financial equations and distribution of assets, benefit allocation - and many other facets and factors as well. On top of all of this, we recognize that you are potentially dealing with all of the emotions that are natural in a divorce case and that you are likely notably concerned about the welfare of you and your children. Our suggestion is that you arm yourself with knowledge and really think through what is important to your welfare for the short and the long term. Share this with your attorney and with any other trusted advisors.

Strategy Session #1…Who Should File First?

Whether you file for divorce before your husband files or you file a cross-claim after he files does not make any difference as far as whether you "win" or "lose." Whether or not you file for divorce first will not affect the substantive outcome of your case. It does affect procedural matters such as who is called the Plaintiff and who is called the Defendant and who puts his or her evidence on first at trial. This may or may not matter to you or your attorney. A more important issue in determining whether to go ahead and file for divorce is whether you need pendente lite relief from the court.

Let's Talk "$$$$"

At this point, you are probably wondering about your entitlements. You want to know what you will receive and how you will be able to support yourself and, if applicable, your children. While you may feel more comfortable about the actual divorce process, you need to understand what to expect financially. So let's talk money.

In order to provide you with the kind of detailed information you are looking for in your particular case, your attorney will need to know the reasons for your divorce, the number of years you and your husband have been married, the number of children you have and their ages, the real-estate you own (and how and when it was acquired), life and health insurance policies you have, and your family assets and liabilities (and particularly if you or your spouse is retired military and there is any subsequent employment). If you are the non-working spouse and your husband is the active duty servicemember, then you will want to put together information about the non-monetary contributions you have made to the household. If you are the active, duty servicemember and you essentially maintain the household, you will certainly want to make sure your attorney knows this as well.

To help you prepare this information, think about what percentage of the following tasks you do and, conversely, what percentage your husband contributes:

- Food Purchaser
- Cook
- Meal Planner
- Infant Caretaker
- Child Care Provider
- Chauffeur
- School Activities Overseer
- Extra Curricular Activities Manager
- Homework Manager for the Children
- Baths/Bedtime Overseer
- Dishwasher
- Maintenance Provider Inside the Home
- Maintenance Provider Outside the Home
- Launderer
- Cleaner
- Gardener
- Lawn Care Maintainer
- Garbage Disposal Custodian
- Clothing Repairperson
- Pet Custodian
- Errand Runner
- Vacation / Move (PCS!) Planner
- Bookkeeper / Budgeter

Spousal Support

In Virginia, there are five types of spousal support awards

available in divorce. The courts are empowered to award any one type of support or any combination of types of support it deems appropriate. The types of support are:

○ Lump sum award;
○ Periodic payments;
○ Rehabilitative support for a fixed period of time;
○ Reservation of right to ask for support at a future time; *and*
○ A combination of some of the above

In determining the appropriateness of spousal support in a final divorce hearing, there are thirteen factors outlined in the spousal support section of the Virginia Code 20-107.1 (see below). It is helpful to go through each of the factors and write out your response to each for your attorney so that any unusual facts can be brought to his or her attention.

The court must consider the following factors to determine spousal support.

Factors

1. *The obligations, needs and financial resources of the parties, including but not limited to income from all pension, profit sharing or retirement plans, of whatever nature;*

2. *The standard of living established during the marriage; *Note—this does not mean that you are entitled to be maintained in the lifestyle to which you become accustomed during the marriage. The reality is that the income that supported the marital household cannot now support two households at the same level. You and your husband will both have to reduce your spending a*

little. However, it is far better to live happily with fewer luxuries than miserably with 800 cable TV channels;

3. *The duration of the marriage;*

4. *The age and physical and mental condition of the parties and any special circumstances of the family;*

5. *The extent to which the age, physical or mental condition or special circumstances of any child of the parties would make it appropriate that a party not seek employment outside of the home;*

6. *The contributions, monetary and non-monetary, of each party to the well-being of the family;*

7. *The property interests of the parties, both real and personal, tangible and intangible;*

8. *The provisions made with regard to the marital property under §§ 20-107.3;*

9. *The earning capacity, including the skills, education and training of the parties and the present employment opportunities for each spouse;*

10. *The opportunity for, ability of, and the time and costs involved for a party to acquire the appropriate education, training and employment to obtain the skills needed to enhance his or her earning ability;*

11. *The decisions regarding employment, career, economics, education and parenting arrangements made by the*

*parties during the marriage and their effect on present
and future earning potential, including the length of time
and reasons why one or both of the parties have been
absent from the job market;*

12. *The extent to which either party has contributed to the
attainment of education, training, career position or
profession of the other party; and*

13. *Such other factors, including the tax consequences to
each party, as are necessary to consider the equities
between the parties.*

Rules of Thumb – Spousal Support

We are routinely asked how long a woman is entitled to
receive support if she qualifies for it. While there are no ab-
solute rules or presumptions in Virginia, one rule of thumb
is helpful. If you have been married five years or fewer, it is
possible that you may not be awarded any support, or you
may be awarded limited support to last no longer than until
your divorce is final or, preferably, the length of your marriage. An award of support for a short marriage still requires
the court to examine all of the factors as detailed above, but
the court is usually reluctant to burden a spouse with long
term spousal support for a short marriage. The award of
support in a short marriage would also require that there
be a significant disparity of income between you and your
spouse.

On the other hand, if you have been married between 6
and 19 years and qualify for support, it would be reasonable
to expect that you would be entitled to support for at least
half the length of your marriage or longer, provided the court
finds that the appropriate factors exist: namely, that you are

not at fault in causing the divorce, and there is an appropriate disparity of income between you and your husband. With a marriage longer than 20 years, absent fault on your part and assuming a disparity of income, one could realistically expect support until death of either party, remarriage of the receiving spouse, or clear and convincing evidence of cohabitation with another in a relationship analogous to marriage for twelve months or longer. Again, support is completely at the discretion of your individual judge and is therefore difficult to predict, but these rules of thumb may help you in settlement negotiations.

So...Tell Me How Much This Is Already!

Once it has been determined that you are entitled to support, the next obvious question is "How much support will I receive?" Unlike child support, there is no statewide formula for support awarded by final divorce decree; however there are formulas used by various courts for temporary support. If you are seeking support in the Juvenile and District Relations Courts, then the Fairfax Guidelines are now applicable by statute.

The formula for the Fairfax guidelines is as follows (if children involved):

A. *Payor's Income x 28 percent; (if no minor children then x 33percent)*
B. *Payee's Income x 58 percent; (if no minor children then x 50percent)*
C. *Line A minus Line B equals proposed Spousal Support*

Some courts around the Commonwealth have determined their own formulas for temporary (pendente lite) support hearings in divorce, and there are formulas in Fairfax, Richmond, and Harrisonburg. Generally, a look at the Fairfax Guidelines is helpful in providing a client a range of spousal support she can expect. HOWEVER, these guidelines are not binding on the Circuit Court, and the issue of spousal support is left to the discretion of the judges, upon application of the statutory factors.

The goals of the court are different at a temporary support hearing early in the divorce versus the awarding of support in the final divorce decree. Early on in a pendente lite hearing where the court has a very limited period of time to hear from witnesses and make determinations, the court's goal is to keep the situation relatively simple and to make an award either by formula as in the Fairfax Guidelines, or based on a general assessment of the income of the parties and their expenses. Because pendente lite support has to be determined in a relatively short period of time, it is generally a function of weighing the income of the parties against their relative expenses without taking into consideration more complex matters that a later court will assess.

Equitable Distribution

How Virginia divides marital property (which includes all material possessions acquired by the parties during the marriage other than separate property) between spouses is determined by Section 20-107.3 of the Code of Virginia. There are three basic types of property in Virginia: **separate** property, **marital** property, and **hybrid** property. The differences amongst these three types of property are very important, and your understanding of them is critical to your understanding of what you may or may not be entitled to in your divorce.

In your court case, it is up to the attorneys to identify all of the property of the marriage and then assist the court with evidence to show whether the property is separate, hybrid or marital. The court assumes that all property acquired during the marriage is marital, unless proven otherwise by one of the parties. The legal definitions of the types of property follow:

Separate property: This includes any property owned by one spouse prior to the marriage or acquired after separation, or property acquired during the marriage by gift or inheritance from someone other than your spouse. Thus, if you had an antique chair that was passed on to you by the death of a family member, that would legally be your chair. Likewise, if your husband inherited $100,000 and kept it separately in an account, and it is now worth $400,000, those are his separate funds.

Marital property: This includes all property, not otherwise separate, acquired during the marriage, regardless of the name on the title. This means that if you husband bought a boat in his name during the marriage, with funds earned during the marriage, the boat is a marital asset, even though it may be legally titled only in his name. Likewise, the gold bracelet that your husband gave you for Christmas as a gift is a marital asset, notwithstanding the fact that it was a gift from him to you. The courts view a marriage as an economic partnership, and all monetary and non-monetary benefits of the husband and wife are to be shared by the parties equitably or as the court deems fairly, which may differ from sharing benefits equally.

Hybrid property: This includes property that is part separate and part marital. An example of this might be that your grandmother left you some money prior to your getting married, and you kept it in a separate account. When buying your first house, you took that money, along with money that you and your husband had saved during the marriage, and you deposited your inheritance into the joint checking account, and then a week later you two went to the closing and paid for the home. In Virginia, if you can trace the origin of the funds and show where they came from and how they were applied, then you can prove the residence is a hybrid property because part of the money came from separate funds and part of the money came from marital funds. There are several ways to determine what percentage of the residence is your separate property and what percentage of the residence is jointly held marital property. How the physical property is titled may not be as important as how the house was funded, unless there was a Deed of Gift from one spouse to both spouses or solely to the other spouse, in which case the Deed of Gift will probably be applied.

Once all the assets and debts of the marriage are identified and the nature of their identity is determined, then it may be necessary to value the assets for the purpose of equitable distribution. Different assets are valued in different ways. For instance, a car's value is its Blue Book figure, whereas a home's value would normally be determined by an appraiser, or a couple may agree to use the city-assessed real estate value. Experts may be called in to determine the value of antiques, unless the parties can agree on their worth. After the assets have been identified, classified, and valued, then the court will determine how those assets are to be distributed between the parties.

Perhaps the most difficult evaluation issue arises from the ownership of a family business or a sole proprietorship. Business evaluation experts are often required to value such assets, adding greatly to the expense of a divorce.

With real estate assets, you are not only valuing the marital residence but you may well have to value vacation homes, timeshares, and interests in rental homes.

The next class of assets is personal property like dishes, lamps, televisions, and furniture. Personal property must be identified and valued before being distributed. Usually we use an auctioneer or estate appraiser to value everyday personal property, unless there are antiques or high value unique personal property.

With regard to personal property, the value is not what you paid for it, but rather what it is worth on the market today. For most people, their personal property will have relatively little value. An example might be the large screen television you originally bought two years ago for several thousand dollars, but which now may only be worth a few hundred dollars due to technological advances. With regard to personal property, it is always less costly and simpler for the couple to try to work out how they are going to share items rather than involving the court or their attorneys. If the parties cannot come to an agreement, there are easy ways to encourage cooperation such as alternating choices after flipping a coin to determine who goes first in selecting personal property.

Once the assets and liabilities are determined and valued, they then must be distributed. The parties can agree on the division of assets or the court will award each asset and liability to one or the other party. If the division of the assets and liabilities cannot be resolved by both parties, the court will order that one person receive the asset and order the receiving party to pay the non-receiving party a monetary award determined by the court - or the court will order all the jointly titled property sold and the money divided between the couple.

Child Custody / Visitation

Custody/visitation is the number one issue for women who have children under the age of 18. The law of custody has gone from favoring mothers as caretakers of young children to being "gender neutral." Either parent of a child starts with no presumption in his or her favor in a custody case. The court undertakes a custody decision by an analysis of a series of factors that, in their entirety, help the court determine the best interest of the child(ren). The factors that govern custody or visitation are outlined in the Code of Virginia and reproduced here.

<u>Virginia Child Custody–Best Interest of the Child–
Va. Code §20-124.3</u>

Section 20-124.3 of the Virginia Code lists a number of factors that the judge should consider in deciding what is in the <u>child's best interests</u>. They are as follows:

1. *The age and physical and mental condition of the child and the child's developmental needs;*

2. *The age and physical and mental condition of each parent;*

3. *The relationship between each parent and the child and the parent's positive involvement and ability to assess and meet the child's needs;*

4. *The child's needs, including important relationships such as with brothers and sisters, grandparents, and other relatives;*

5. *The role which each parent has played and will play in the upbringing and care of the child;*

6. *The propensity of each parent to actively support the child's contact and relationship with the other parent, including whether a parent has unreasonably denied the other parent access to visitation with the child. (Note: The courts seem to give extra weight to this factor);*

7. *Both parent's willingness to support the child's relationship with the other parent, their willingness and ability to maintain a close relationship with the child, and their ability to cooperate in matters affecting the child;*

8. *The child's preference (the weight of this will depend on the age and maturity of the child. There is no age at which a minor child can be the one who decides);*

9. *Any history of family abuse as that term is defined in Section 16.1-288 or sexual abuse. If the court finds such a history, the court may disregard the factors in number 6 above; and*

10. *Any other factors the judge may feel necessary to consider.*

There are basically two types of custody: **Legal and Physical**. Legal custody determines who has the right to make major decisions affecting how your child is going to be raised. Normally, the courts award joint legal custody, which essentially means that both parents will jointly make major decisions regarding the child. The major decisions contemplated involve education, religion and non-emergency medical care.

Obviously, the child is going to go to the emergency room if a medical emergency arises and will continue to have regular check-ups. Joint decisions include those concerning medication, medical care or elective surgery. If one parent wants one outcome and the other one does not, then the courts may have to determine what care the child will receive.

Sole legal custody means that one parent has the right to make all decisions regarding the child, except for decisions that are otherwise ordered by the court. Sole legal custody is not normally awarded unless the parties agree, or if there is child abuse, drug abuse, or some major problem which adversely affects the child such as two parents who cannot work together for the sake of the child.

Once the decision has been rendered as to sole legal custody or joint legal custody, the court then turns its attention to the issue of physical custody. Physical custody determines with whom the child resides. Physical custody rulings concern the amount of time the child spends with each parent. If the child has more than ninety overnight twenty four hour visits with each parent, this is referred to as shared custody. One of the issues inherent with shared custody is the fact that child support is based, in part, on the custodial arrangement and particularly when both parents have more than ninety days of overnight visitation lasting 24 hours. The child support paid to the parent who has the most time with the child is often reduced due to shared custody support guidelines, since the other parent likewise has financial responsibilities for the child's care.

Another form of custody is known as split custody, where one or more children live with one parent and another child or children live primarily with the other parent. While the courts do not favor split custody, there are times when the children are deemed better off being split between the parents. Parenting time can be scheduled so that the children living in different households can spend time together with a certain frequency each month.

The most important advice we suggest to women regarding custody is to recognize that each family is different and there is no "right" custodial arrangement. What works for one family may not work for the next. What is clear however, is that children appear to do better when they have time with each parent so long as they have two good parents.

There are many issues involved in the custodial realm which need to be discussed in detail with your attorney. The issue of relocation is of concern to the courts because any such move interferes with the ability of the child to have a satisfactory relationship with the other parent. Grandparent rights, the rights of step-parents, and legal emancipation of a child before attaining the age of eighteen are also very important issues that parents face and which require clear guidance from both mental health professionals and attorneys.

When dealing with parenting issues, it is important for the parents to figure out how to communicate with one another in their rearranged family structure. Divorce need not be the destruction of a family relationship, but merely a rearrangement of how the family works.

With regard to relocation, the court requires that each parent give thirty days' advance written notice to the court and to the other parent if one intends to relocate or change his or her address. The custodial parent's choice to relocate can often be a reason for the court to change custody, so you should consult with your attorney before considering a move.

Each parent has the right of access to the academic, medical, hospital, or other health records of that parent's minor child, unless it is otherwise ordered by the court for cause shown.

IMPORTANT -
THE CARDINAL RULES ABOUT CUSTODY

1. "The best interest of the child" is the guiding principle in custody cases. Because the best interest of the child means something different to every participant in a custody trial, be aware that your point of view will not necessarily be the same as the judge's.

2. We recommend that you always refer to the children as "our" children, not "my" children or "my" child as this shows maturity and reasonableness in court.

3. We highly urge that you never, ever, ever talk disparagingly about the child's father to, or in the presence of, one of your children. If your child asks you a question and the honest answer requires you to address a less than flattering aspect of your spouse, we encourage you to speak to your child's therapist about how to best respond.

4. The court knows that you and your husband may diverge in your philosophies of how to raise the children. The court realizes that you likely differ in how you believe rules should be enforced, how punishment should be given, and how children should be treated. The court does not intend to favor one parenting style over the other, so try and communicate and work with your soon-to-be ex. If you cannot communicate with your husband about the children, then we recommend that you talk with a children's

mental health expert about how to handle specific issues.

5. If you believe that you are going to be in a contested custody case, we urge you to see an attorney experienced in contested custody cases immediately, so this person can give you sage advice on what to do, and just as importantly, what not to do.

6. Be aware that courts look disapprovingly at restricting access to a child. Possibly the biggest reason a father would win custody is if the mother has custody and restricts the child's access to his father.

7. Introducing new boyfriends and girlfriends into the life of a child before being divorced is potentially dangerous and damaging to your child and therefore to your custody case. Short answer: Don't do it!

8. Unless the father is abusive, allow and encourage your child to have a picture of him in the child's room.

9. Never deny visitation because you have not received the child support check. In the eyes of the court, the two are not directly related and it is deemed unreasonable to deny visitation even to a nonpaying father.

10. Custody is about CHILDREN, not fault.

11. Never, ever, move out and temporarily leave your children with their dad unless you are prepared for him to be awarded custody of them.

12. Don't move out with the children unless you have a detailed plan of action coordinated with your attorney.

13. If you are in a romantic relationship, do not have your romantic partner spend the night when the children are there, even if you think they don't know because they are asleep.

14. Even if your husband's weekends with the children are your first nights off in years, resist the urge to jump start your social life and/or heal your broken heart by frequent late nights out. This will likely be used against you if you end up in a custody battle.

15. Do not let off steam by venting to your children's teachers, coaches, etc., about your ex. You do not want to appear as "the angry ex" in court.

Good custody lawyers have access to various technologies which can aid them and you in preparing for your custody case. Ask your custody lawyer, or divorce lawyer, to demonstrate to you the various technologies they have available to help you win your case.

Aside from your attorney, the internet is the number one provider of information to fathers trying to obtain custody. One merely has to Google "father's rights" or "children's rights" to see the incredible amount of information that is available online to parents. Your divorce attorney should be able to provide you with credible websites that will help you in your case.

Strategy Session #2 -
Custody for the Active Duty Servicemember

With the increased operational tempo of the United States Military over the past 10 years, more and more mothers with custody are facing the daunting situation of what to do with their child(ren) during deployments and how to handle moves under Permanent Change of Station orders. In Part III, we will discuss this topic in greater depth. Suffice it say, this issue needs to be on your radar when you are talking to your attorney. If you can work out an agreement in your separation agreement or early on with your ex - this is far better than leaving the issue undecided for a state court judge to decide in an emergency situation. The best case scenario is to arrange a transfer of custody from the deploying military parent to the other parent by means of a consent order prior to the military parent's deployment. This order can detail the circumstances of the transfer and outline the specific dates or departure, expected date of return, educational care, and any other custodial arrangements and care. It also should make it absolutely clear that your child(ren) will be immediately returned to you without the need to return to court to request relief.

You may have also heard of the Servicemembers Civil Relief Act ("SCRA"). Signed in 2003, the SCRA was designed to protect those on active duty – but it also affords protection for Reservists and members of the National Guard. One of the major benefits to deployed servicemembers under the SCRA is the ability to suspend a civil court case until they are able to participate. This is known as a "stay of proceeding"– and what it can simply mean to you is "delay." In some cases (again, very fact-specific and depending on the jurisdiction), temporary custody can trump the SCRA. **CAUTION**: In the event you wish to have someone other than the biological father look after your child(ren) if you are called up for deployment/mobilization, you need to discuss this with your attorney and plan accordingly.

Child Support

Virginia has adopted a child support model that is formulaic and is based on the number of children and the relative incomes of the parties. The statutes governing child support in the Virginia Code are Sections 20-108.1, .2, and 20-107.2. If you are interested in determining how child support is calculated, please go to www.dss.virginia.gov/family/dcse_calc.cgi. For purposes of determining child support, we have included a child support guideline worksheet (page 66) and filled in an example of how it works with the mother making $2000 per month and the father making $6000 per month. In our example, the wife receives $520 spousal support, there are two children and the monthly amount of healthcare coverage paid by the father through his employer for just the children's portion is $150 per month. Child care is after school and costs approximately $120 per month. Based on those factors, as worked out in the child support guidelines, child support is $1006 per month. The court can deviate from the guidelines in special circumstances, but this is highly unusual.

COMBINED SUPPORT WORKSHEET   v. _____

Fairfax Guideline Spousal and Child Support

Complaint No. _____

Worksheet of: _____   Date: _____

Child support is payable for: **2** children.   Ages: _____

A. GROSS INCOME OF PARTIES

	Mother/Wife	Father/Husband
1. Monthly Gross Income of Each Party:	$2,000	$6,000
2. Adjustment for Support of "Other Children":		
3. Adjustment for Self-Employment Tax:		
4. Adjusted Gross Incomes of Parties:	$2,000	$6,000
5. Combined Adjusted Income:	**$8,000**	

B. SPOUSAL SUPPORT

Payor Spouse
- ● Husband
- ○ Wife

1. Payor Spouse's Adjusted Income:	$6,000	
2. Payor's Income X 28%		$1,680
3. Payee Spouse's Adjusted Income:	$2,000	
4. Payee's Income X 58%		$1,160
5. Guideline Spousal Support: (Line 2 Minus Line 4):		
6. Proposed Adjustments to Spousal Support:		

Guideline Spousal Support
$520

Uses The 28% - 58% Fairfax (§16.1-278.17) Guideline Formula.

7. Proposed Spousal Support Payable to: **Wife**

Adjusted Spousal Support
$520

C. CHILD SUPPORT

Incomes with Guideline Adjustments including Spousal Support

Custodian
- ● Mother
- ○ Father

	Combined	Mother	Father
Adjusted Gross Incomes:	$8,000	$2,520	$5,480
		Income Shares	
Each Party's Percent of Combined Gross Income:		31.5%	68.5%
1. Schedule Amount for Basic Child Support:			$1,418
2. Work-related Child Care Costs:			$120
3. Medical Insurance for Child/Children:			$150
4. Total Child Support Need (Sum: 1+2+3+4):			

$1,418 From Support Table

Child Support Need
$1,688

	Mother	Father
5. Child Support Obligation of Each Party:		
(Total support need X Income Share):	$532	$1,156
6. Direct Payment of Medical Insurance:		($150)
7. Each Party's Presumptive Guideline Share:	$532	$1,006
8. Guideline Child Support Payable to:	**Mother**	
9. Proposed Deviations From Guideline Support:		
10. Each Party's Proposed Share:	$532	$1,006
11. Proposed Adjusted Child Support Payable to:	**Mother**	

Guideline Child Support
$1,006

Adjusted Child Support
$1,006

D. Net Child and Spousal Support, Payable To: Wife/Mother

NET SUPPORT
$1,526

Submitted by: _____
Counsel for: _____

Retirements

In Virginia, there is a formula to divide military pensions. On the other hand, deferred contribution plans such as 401(K) plans are divided by determining the marital share of the account and dividing that. The critical dates are the date of the marriage and the date of separation. The formula for retirements is as follows: the numerator (number on top) is the total number of years that husband/wife was employed as a servicemember during the marriage to the date of separation. The denominator (or bottom number) is the total number of years employed as a servicemember. That is multiplied by 50 percent times benefit received (or amount in the account).

Virginia Formula for Military

Number of years employed by the military during
the marriage to date of separation   X   50 percent   X   Amount of Monthly Benefit
Total number of years husband has been or was employed by the military

If husband is still employed, this number is unknown and we will use "Z" for "unknown."

EXAMPLE: $3,000 monthly Pension Payment
10 years of marriage to date of separation
20 years of employment

$\frac{10}{20}$ x 50percent x $3,000

5/10 x 50percent x $3,000 =
½   x .50 x $3,000 =
.25 x $3,000 = $750.00 per month.

There are issues such as what date one uses to value pensions and 401Ks that require more detailed discussion with your attorney.

Taxes. There are many tax implications regarding actions taken during a divorce which are not discussed in this book. We recommend that you address tax implications carefully with your attorney and with your accountant to prevent unneeded deductions or charges and to maximize your entitlements. Generally, spousal support is taxable to the recipient and deductible by the payor. Child support, on the other hand, is generally non-taxable to the recipient and non-deductible by the payor.

3 THE NITTY-GRITTY OF YOUR MILITARY DIVORCE

Ok, now you can take a deep breath and relax. We have just gone through all of the major aspects of a divorce case in Virginia. You have heard about the court system, filing and serving paperwork, realistic expectations of the nature of the process, and the issues that tend to loom large and affect litigation in the majority of divorce cases. There won't be any more information or discussion on the general legal process from here on out. What we will discuss next are the <u>military-specific aspects</u> of your case. After reading Part III, you will be exposed to many of the more intricate concepts of a military-specific divorce and you will gain an even greater, in-depth vocabulary of many of the concepts and terms along the way. After reading this section, you will be as familiar as many Virginia attorneys with military-specific divorce topics and you will be able to properly interview a prospective attorney and decide if he or she is qualified to handle your military-specific divorce!

Servicemembers Civil Relief Act (SCRA)

While most folks have heard of the SCRA and the passing of this major legislation in 2003, what few recall is that its predecessor–the "Soldiers' and Sailors' Civil Relief Act" (SCCRA), has been around since 1940. The SCRA was essentially drafted to update the SCCRA and incorporate many of the judicial decisions that have been decided about the SCCRA over the prior 60 plus years.

As previously mentioned, the SCRA was signed into law to protect those on active duty, as well as Reservists and members of the National Guard. The SCRA is closely adhered to by the courts and, in most instances, benefits deploying servicemembers. You also should know that the SCRA is an extremely broad document – and deals with literally thousands of issues that servicemembers may face. We are really only looking into it from a divorce perspective – and sometimes this can be difficult to understand, particularly when the SCRA is invoked to your detriment.

The SCRA is a "Shield", Not a "Sword"

The best way to explain how the SCRA works is to use the sword/shield analogy. If someone is trying to litigate an issue in court to your detriment - and you cannot get into court due to your mobilization/deployment, the court will allow you to use the SCRA (as a shield) to delay the proceedings until you can properly appear. What you cannot do is attempt to do something nefarious (using the SCRA as a sword) and then prohibit your spouse from coming into court for relief by claiming that you are unable to appear due to your deployment and that the case should be delayed until your return.

Let's talk about a bit more about a mobilization situation. If you are being called up to deploy and you are the custodial parent, do not fall into the trap of believing the SCRA will assist you in delaying your case or allow you to inappropriately alter your child's custody arrangement. Let's also say that you have a shared custody arrangement with your ex, but now that you know you are deploying, you want this child to be in the custody of someone else. More likely than not, your ex will bring you into court to attempt to enforce the custody arrangement, and even if there isn't one, he will claim that he is entitled to custody as the biological parent – AND he may also petition the court for Pendente Lite relief that you may be obligated to pay. If you try to stay the proceedings under the SCRA without just cause, the court will likely not grant you this delay and the case will proceed with or without you. The court will not likely delay this unresolved situation with regard to your child's life simply because you are a servicemember and you and your ex can't get along.

Powers of Attorney and Separation Agreements

As anyone on active duty knows, it is relatively easy (and free!) to get a Power of Attorney for literally anything by walking into a Base Legal Assistance Office. Practically any JAG attorney or active duty paralegal can recall numerous instances of deploying sailors, soldiers, airmen and Marines wanting to sign a Power of Attorney to allow their significant other access to their bank accounts or to empower their spouse with the ability to buy, sell, or rent real estate on their behalf. A Power of Attorney is NOT a good idea to transfer custody of your child to someone else, particularly a non-parent - especially if there is a court order that details the custody arrangement. Sometimes this can be confusing - particularly if a superior in your Chain of Command directs you to develop a Family Care Plan and sends you over to the Base Legal Office to fill out various Powers of Attorney forms.

A better way to go about dealing with this situation BEFORE it happens, particularly if you are the active duty servicemember, is to be thinking about mobilization before you agree to a separation agreement. If your attorney is contemplating drafting a custody order or separation agreement - and you are also hoping to later incorporate the document into your final divorce decree - you should specifically have a clause that details who should be designated as the alternate custodian in the event you are called up for deployment on an "unaccompanied" tour (or a tour where you are not allowed to bring dependents). This person may likely be your soon-to-be ex husband. To take this one step further, we also recommend you name an additional alternate custodian in your separation agreement in the event your primary alternate custodian is unwilling or unable to serve as custodian. It is also helpful to then have both parties to the agreement stipulate that this secondary alternate custodian is a fit and proper person to accept the role of secondary alternate custodian.

UCCJEA and UIFSA

With frequent moves and overseas assignments, interstate (and even international) child custody and child support situations arise. These issues can get very complicated very quickly. If you are embroiled in an international or inter-state child custody issue, you should speak with an attorney immediately who not only is well versed in child custody cases, but also one who has a very good understanding of the military. There are two major federal laws that may affect your divorce or custody case and you want to make sure your attorney understands how these laws may impact your case, now and in the future.

First - The UCCJEA and Home State

The Uniform Child Custody Jurisdiction and Enforcement Act (UCCJEA) vests "exclusive and continuing jurisdiction" for initial child custody litigation in the courts of the child's "home state," which is defined as the state where the child has lived with a parent for six consecutive months prior to the commencement of the proceeding (or since birth for children younger than six months). If the child has not lived in any state for at least six months, then a court in a state that has (1) "significant connections" with the child and at least one parent and (2) "substantial evidence concerning the child's care, protection, training, and personal relationships" that has been established will likely become the child custody jurisdiction. If more than one state has "significant connections" *and* "substantial evidence...," the courts of those states must communicate and determine which state has the most significant connections to the child.

Second - Child Custody Modification Jurisdiction

The reason why this is important is that once a Virginia court has made a child custody determination consistent with the UCCJEA, Virginia will have exclusive, continuing jurisdiction over the child custody matter unless or until the court determines that you or the child no longer have a significant connection to Virginia. So, for example, if your divorce case is adjudicated here in Virginia and your ex-spouse moves to Florida, if he wishes to modify the custody arrangement, he would need to file in a Virginia court - as long as you and the child remain in Virginia. If you subsequently relocate to another state due to remarriage or employment then, after six months, jurisdiction regarding your child(ren) is subject to change and you need to know how to handle this.

This can also be important particularly if you are a female, active duty servicemember and you move out of Virginia on PCS orders down the road. The overarching concept with UCCJEA is that once a custody determination has been made, a court of another state does not have authority to modify the determination, unless the state with jurisdiction determines that it no longer has jurisdiction, or any state court determines that the child, parents, and any acting parents do not reside in the state which currently has jurisdiction.

Now - UIFSA

The Uniform Interstate Family Support Act (UIFSA) functions much the same way; however, it deals with child support modifications (and not child custody like UCCJEA). UIFSA supports the concept that once a Virginia court has entered a child support order, every other state is required to defer to the Virginia courts on this matter. The place where the order was originally entered holds continuing exclusive jurisdiction - and only the laws of that state can be applied to requests to modify the order of child support, unless the original Virginia court loses jurisdiction under the Act.

If you believe that you (and your children) will likely remain in Virginia for the foreseeable future, it is typically in your best interest to have your related claims adjudicated by a court here in the Commonwealth. Not only will the Virginia court system then have continuing exclusive jurisdiction, but also it will be cheaper for you to defend against any later legal actions that may arise. Consider not only having to pay to defend a modification action in court, but in addition having to hire an attorney in another state and then having to travel there to adjudicate the modification case.

The Hague Convention

INTERNATIONAL CAUTION: The concept of international custody may arise and is a complicated area. You should know that the UCCJEA will treat international courts with deference if they have ruled on a child custody situation. In other words, if a foreign country's court has ruled under factual circumstances that conform with the jurisdiction standards of the UCCJEA, that foreign court will be treated as if it were a court of a state in the United States–and that custody order will be enforced. This is another reason to have your case adjudicated here in Virginia if you intend to remain here.

It is also important to mention "The Hague Convention on the Civil Aspects of International Child Abduction." This is a multilateral treaty governing the enforcement of judgments entered by one nation's legal authorities in other nations who were also signatories of the treaty. This treaty was ratified by the United States in 1986 and made effective as federal law in the International Child Abduction Remedies Act in 1988. The Hague Convention was drafted to ensure the prompt return of children who have been abducted from their country of "habitual" or ordinary residence, or wrongfully retained in another country – not their country of residence.

The primary intention of the Convention is to preserve whatever custody arrangement existed immediately before the wrongful removal of the child and thereby deter a parent from crossing international boundaries in search of a more sympathetic court. This applies only to children under the age of 16. The importance of this treaty is that it mandates the return of any child who was a resident of the United States before any action is taken on the custody dispute by the other country, provided that county is also a signatory to this treaty. It also provides that the court in which a Hague Convention action is filed should not consider the merits of any underlying child custody dispute, but rather should only determine that there is another more proper country in whose courts this issue should be heard AND should act expeditiously in making that decision to ease the return of the child.

THERE IS NO MILITARY EXCEPTION TO THE HAGUE CONVENTION! You need to be particularly cautious if you are returning to the United States with a child from overseas and have decided to separate from your husband. A child who is born overseas and has lived there for a period of time until removed by a parent – may be considered to be a habitual resident of that country – and this may cause you difficulty in settling a custody dispute. You also do not want to be accused of child abduction if you remove the child from the other country to the United States without working through this issue properly. You may also want to consult with the nearest Military Legal Assistance Office as most major bases have an attorney who specializes in "host nation" issues.

Military Retirement Benefits

Perhaps the most complicated item to adjudicate in any military divorce case is how to allocate Military Retirement Benefits. First, you need to determine all of the retirement benefits that your servicemember spouse (or you as the active duty servicemember) participate(d) in / or are eligible for. All branches of the armed services participate in a unified retirement system. In addition to the military pension (a defined benefit plan), military personnel may also participate in the Thrift Savings Plan (TSP)– and don't forget about reservist retirement, Medical Care, Commissary Privileges, Education Benefits - and even the Survivor Benefit Plan (SBP). Finally, if a retirement is pending, don't forget to think about Accrued Leave! If your spouse is approaching 20 years of service, but hasn't reached the 20-year mark yet, you definitely want to consult with an attorney before filing a divorce action. You could lose many benefits that you would otherwise be entitled to if you become divorced shortly before your husband reaches 20-years of service. Be very careful if your husband is active duty and you have been married 18 or 19 years of this active duty service.

As you know, retirement for enlisted personnel, warrant officers, and commissioned officers is earned after twenty years of active duty service. To compute the amount of retired pay, first you must determine when your servicemember husband (or you) came on active duty. If this date was sometime between 1980 and 1986, the "High-3" formula is used to compute retired pay (10 U.S.C. §1407(a), 1409(b) (2)). Without going into the specifics of the formula[1], the retired pay is based on the average of the last 36 months pay before retirement.

Redux Retirement and the Career Status Bonus

If your servicemember husband (or you) commenced active duty after August 1, 1986, then there are two options for retirement: either 1) the "High-3" formula discussed above, or 2) what is commonly referred to as REDUX[2]. If REDUX is chosen, you should most certainly consult with an attorney - because what REDUX means is that a mid-career bonus of $30,000 was paid between the servicemember's 14.5 and 15 years of service with a promise by the servicemember to remain on active duty until 20 years. This is known as the Career Status Bonus - and it affects the retired pay because monthly retired pay under REDUX is calculated at 40 percent of the average of the highest three years of basic pay after twenty years of creditable service. The reduction that produces this 40 percent multiplier is computed by subtracting one percent for each full year that the servicemember's

[1] which is incidentally, 2.5 percent x years of service x average of highest 36 months of basic pay
[2] 37 U.S.C.S. § 322(a)(2)

total creditable service is less than 30 years. servicemembers then receive 3.5 percent increases (to the 40 percent multiplier) per year for each additional year served up to the 30 years of active service.

So, for example, under REDUX, a servicemember retiring at 24 years of service gets a 54 percent multiplier. Someone who served on active duty for 30 years would get a 75 percent multiplier. To make matters even more complicated - once the servicemember reaches the age of 62, the Department of Defense recalculates a REDUX retiree's benefit and the servicemember then receives equal monthly pension payments as a High-3 earner would.

Without getting overly complicated - if your soon-to-be ex is a Reservist or National Guardsmen, you need to know that as a member of the Reserves, he too, has a retirement system. As a Reservist, his retirement is different and he will not be eligible for retirement until 60 years of age. What you need most to remember - is how many "points" are involved in this service and when the servicemember entered military service. We are not going to go into the specifics of the Reservist formulas (there are 2), but the Reservist is entitled to retirement after 20 years of creditable service and attaining a sufficient amount of points. The National Guard and the Reserves mail an annual points statement each year to your husband. If your soon-to-be ex (or his attorney) tells you he can't ascertain how many points he has acquired, then you know he is not being forthcoming.

The Ten Year Myth: Confusing Pension Entitlements with Direct Pay

One of the most callous lawyer tricks attempted by an opposing counsel was a letter sent to a servicemember's wife stating, "As you know, the government will not pay you any part of your husband's retirement pension because you have not been married to him for 10 years." The letter was a purposeful misinformation effort to make the wife believe that what her husband had been saying to her for years was true, that she "was not entitled" to any of his retirement pay.

Here are the facts: state law determines what, if any, portion of your husband's retirement pension you are entitled to receive, whether you have been married for 5 years or for 30 of his military career. You have a right to ask for your marital share of his military pension.

Here is where the 10-year rule applies - the government has a rule that it does not have to pay you **directly** your marital share of the pension unless you have been married to your husband for more than 10 years of his military career. Thus, if you were married to him for 8 years of his military career and the court awards you your marital share of his retirement, the payment will come from your husband, not directly from the government. You certainly can seek a voluntary allotment, or, even better, a voluntary irrecoverable allotment from your husband but you don't have the right to direct pay unless you pass the 10-year marriage threshold of military marriage.

So, now that you are getting a handle on how to determine how much income your spouse will receive upon retirement, you must then turn to the Uniformed Services Former Spouses' Protection Act ("USFSPA"). This Act was passed by Congress and is codified at 10 U.S.C. §1408. It is the governing document that allows a state court to divide military retired pay incident to a divorce AND it leaves a lot open for the state to decide. Unfortunately, nowhere in this Act does it give the courts a clear understanding of how to divide the pay. <u>The state court can order the direct pay of a pension award through the Defense Finance and Accounting</u>

Service (DFAS) when there is ten years' overlap between the marriage and creditable military service (10 U.S.C. §1408(d)(2)). However, such direct payments may not exceed 50% of the servicemember's disposable retired pay.

The good news beyond all of this, is that Virginia law pretty much governs the rest of pension divisions. The best practice is to agree on the division of the pension in the Separation Agreement (if possible) and follow up with a Military Pension Division Order or Administrative Domestic Relations Order (ADRO). But always remember that there are other issues to consider when agreeing to a division of assets. Therefore, it is extremely important to gather all relevant information for your attorney before entering into negotiations. You do not want to leave out assets such as the Survivor Benefit Plan and the Thrift Savings Plan. Let's discuss these next...but before we do so, a few other cautionary words are in order. If your servicemember spouse is going to be receiving Military Disability Retired Pay or VA Disability Benefits, be sure to alert your attorney about this. Informing your attorney is very important because Military Disability Retired Pay is excluded under USFSPA and VA Disability Benefits are not subject to property division under USFSPA. And, in some instances, the servicemember can elect to receive disability benefits by waiving the same amount of retired pay - which yields a net increase in pay because the VA portion of monthly compensation is tax-free. Also, if your soon-to-be ex already resides in a state other than Virginia, make sure you alert your attorney to his out-of-state residency because litigating a military pension division outside of the person's domicile (without consent) can be a particularly thorny issue. It may cause part of your case to be dismissed. **Reminder:** the issue of military retirement benefits is complicated and make sure you have a highly qualified advisor review your situation.

Survivor Benefit Plan

Your servicemember ex-spouse (or you as the service-member) will receive pension benefits until his death. This means of course, that the pension benefits stop once the servicemember dies - regardless if the ex-spouse remains living and was receiving a portion or those benefits. So the military created a program for servicemember's spouses to continue retirement pay following the death of the servicemember. It is called a Survivor Benefit Plan (SBP).

The Survivor Benefit Plan ("SBP") is an annuity program that allows retired (or retirement-eligible) active duty service-members to provide continued income to specified beneficiaries at the time of the participant's death (10 U.S.C. §1448). A servicemember may select spouse or former spouse coverage, coverage for the spouse or former spouse and qualifying children, or simply coverage for the qualifying children only. This program is not free...it is paid out of the retiree's paycheck. (Therefore, it is important to recognize that this payment for SBP will reduce the servicemember's pension income - and, hence, potentially your share of it!). The cost of SBP will depend on the type of coverage selected and the base amount chosen. According to 10 U.S.C. § 1447(6), the base amount may be any amount between $300 and the full amount of the servicemember's monthly retired pay. In very general terms, the premium rate for former spouse coverage is 6.5 percent of the selected base amount. The designated survivor would then receive a lifetime annuity of 55 percent of the designated base amount.

BASIC SBP CALCULATIONS BASED ON: **$3,000 per month retired pay:**

Maximum Payout to surviving ex-spouse: $1,650 (55percent of retired pay)
Premium Cost: $195 per month ($3,000 x 6.5 percent)

DO NOT SIGN ANY DOCUMENTS WITHOUT TALK-ING WITH AN ATTORNEY!

There is no simple answer as to whether or not you and your attorney should negotiate for SBP coverage. Also, know that life insurance may be a cheaper alternative although not necessarily a better option. Among the issues we would discuss with you is your financial situation. In the event that your spouse or ex-spouse dies and the pension benefits were to stop, do you have adequate income from all other sources to handle your loss of pension income? Our standard position is to insist on SBP, since we have seen far too many insurance companies fail. We will still bet on the U.S. Government's solvency versus a private insurance carrier's solvency. While SBP may be somewhat costly, it does not require that either you or your spouse undergo a physical exam, unlike the requirements of many life insurance companies. Another advantage is that your husband cannot terminate SBP coverage without your consent. However, you should know that once SBP is elected, it cannot be cancelled. There are no returns of premiums paid if you die before your husband, and it has no equity build-up or cash surrender value like some life insurance policies.

This is a lot to take in and consider on top of everything else. Understanding the concept and the pros and cons of SBP, however, is a very good start as you enter negotiations with your soon-to-be ex. You might also consider adding a life insurance clause in case your ex-spouse dies while child support or college expenses are still due. Life Insurance is beyond the scope of this book, but it is a topic that goes hand-in-hand with SBP benefits and it is certainly worth discussing with your attorney.

Thrift Savings Plan

Another component of your servicemember's benefits is the Thrift Savings Plan ("TSP"). Think about the TSP as a government "401 K" plan which, if funded by your husband during the marriage, is a marital asset to be divided upon divorce whether your husband qualifies for a pension or not. Contributions to TSP are taken from pre-tax dollars and the earnings on these contributions are tax-deferred. Therefore, the servicemember does not pay income taxes on contributions or earnings unless or until the funds are withdrawn.

You should be aware that after December 2005, a servicemember has had the option of signing up and contributing up to 100 percent of his or her basic pay and other compensation all pre-tax. Servicemembers can also contribute to their TSP special, incentive or hazardous pay up to a total of $15,000 annually. There are also other rules about contributions earned while in a combat zone, which are found on the website www.tsp.gov. Some important items to remember about TSP as you consider divorce are as follows:

1. Do not forget about this retirement benefit during your settlement negotiations.

2. Gather as much documentation and provide it to your attorney. You should attempt to ascertain how much is in your husband's Thrift Savings Plan, if he has used this benefit. If he has opened an account, be sure to know how much he contributed during the marriage.

3. A court order is required to divide the funds in a servicemember's TSP.

4. For a complete explanation of the Thrift Savings Plan, see the TSP home page: www.tsp.gov.

Medical Benefits and Commissary / Exchange Privileges

You may have heard some of your friends or even an attorney refer to a 20/20/20 spouse. This simply means refers to at least 20 years of military service, 20 years of marriage AND 20 years of overlap between the two; i.e, you were married for 20 years of his active duty service years. This is important because if you are such a spouse, then you are entitled to full military medical care, including TRICARE, if you are not enrolled in an employer-sponsored health plan. This also means you are entitled to Commissary and Exchange privileges. IT IS IMPORTANT TO REMEMBER THAT THIS APPLIES TO UN-REMARRIED FORMER SPOUSES – AND IT IS CURRENTLY FOR LIFE!

There is also something called a 20/20/15 spouse. This refers to 20 years of military service, 20 years of marriage, and between 15 but less than 20 years of overlap between the two. If you qualify as a 20/20/15 spouse, you can receive full military medical care, including TRICARE, for a period of one year from the date of divorce - provided you are not enrolled in an employer-sponsored health plan.

A former spouse who qualifies for either of the above may apply for an ID card at any military ID card facility. You would need to fill out DD Form 1172 and bring a valid picture ID card, a copy of your marriage certificate, the court decree, a statement detailing the military spouse's service, and a statement documenting the fact that you are not remarried and that you are not participating in an employer-sponsored health care plan.

This information is important for two reasons. First, if you are the servicemember, there is an inherent value in the above and it can be mentioned during the negotiations with your husband. Secondly, if you are married to a servicemember, and your soon-to-be ex-husband is approaching 20 years of active military service, you may wish to defer, delay, or negotiate an agreement that provides that no divorce will occur before you qualify for 20/20/20 or 20/20/15 status. Be careful with this! You want to discuss this strategy with your attorney before alerting your husband to your wishes. (See Summary Chart of Former Spouse Benefits on page 117.)

Educational Benefits - GI Bill[3]

As of August 1, 2009, servicemembers enrolled in the Post-9/11 GI Bill program are able to transfer unused educational benefits to their spouses or children. It is important to note, a subsequent divorce will not affect the transferee's eligibility to receive educational benefits, HOWEVER, after an individual has designated a spouse as a transferee under this section, the eligible individual retains the right to revoke or modify the transfer at any time. This is the important point you will want to discuss with your attorney.

Eligibility

Any member of the Armed Forces (active duty or Selected Reserve, officer or enlisted) on or after August 1, 2009, is eligible for the Post-9/11 GI Bill if one of the following conditions applies: he or she

- ○ Has at least 6 years of service in the Armed Forces on the date of election and agrees to serve 4 additional years in the Armed Forces from the date of election.
- ○ Has at least 10 years of service in the Armed Forces (active duty and/or selected reserve) on the date of election, is precluded by either standard policy (service or DoD) or statute from committing to 4 additional years, and agrees to serve for the maximum amount of time allowed by such policy or statute, or

[3] *Information taken from Department of Veterans Affairs website at:*
http://gibill.va.gov/post-911/post-911-gi-bill-summary/transfer-of-benefits.html

o   Is or becomes retirement eligible during the period from August 1, 2009, through August 1, 2013. A servicemember is considered to be retirement eligible if he or she has completed 20 years of active duty or 20 qualifying years of reserve service.
o   For those individuals eligible for retirement on August 1, 2009, no additional service is required.
o   For those individuals who have an approved retirement date after August 1, 2009, and before July 1, 2010, no additional service is required.
o   For those individuals eligible for retirement after August 1, 2009, and before August 1, 2010, 1 year of additional service after approval of transfer is required.
o   For those individuals eligible for retirement on or after August 1, 2010, and before August 1, 2011, 2 years of additional service after approval of transfer are required.
o   For those individuals eligible for retirement on or after August 1, 2011, and before August 1, 2012, 3 years of additional service after approval of transfer required.

Eligible Dependents - GI Bill

An individual approved to transfer an entitlement to educational assistance under this section may transfer the individual's entitlement to
o   The individual's spouse;
o   One or more of the individual's children;
o   Any combination of spouse and child; or
o   A family member must be enrolled in the Defense Eligibility Enrollment Reporting System (DEERS) and be eligible for benefits, at the time of transfer to receive transferred educational benefits.

Nature of Transfer - GI Bill

An eligible servicemember may transfer up to the total months of unused Post-9/11 GI Bill benefits, or the entire 36 months if the member has used none. Family members use of transferred educational benefits is subject to the certain qualifications. For the spouse, the following pertain:

o   He or she may start to use the benefit immediately;

o   He or she may use the benefit while the member remains in the Armed Forces or after separation from active duty;

o   He or she is not eligible for the monthly stipend or books and supplies stipend while the member is serving on active duty;

o   He or she can use the benefit for up to 15 years after the servicemember's last separation from active duty.

For a child, the following conditions pertain:

o   He or she may start to use the benefit only after the individual making the transfer has completed at least 10 years of service in the Armed Forces;

o   He or she may use the benefit while the eligible individual remains in the Armed Forces or after separation from active duty;

o   He or she may not use the benefit until having attained a secondary school diploma (or equivalency certificate), or reached 18 years of age;

o   He or she is entitled to the monthly stipend and books and supplies stipend even though the eligible individual is on active duty; and

o   He or she is not subject to the 15-year delimiting date but may not use the benefit after reaching 26 years of age.

Family Advocacy Program

Well, we have discussed many of the military-specific details that can affect your divorce outcome markedly. It is important to note that we did not exhaust every conceivable military-specific issue that could arise in your divorce. However, we discussed the most significant issues that may arise so that you are informed about military divorce topics. There is one remaining topic that we would like to discuss as we conclude our book. If you are in the unfortunate situation of being involved in an abusive relationship, whether it be physical, sexual, or emotional abuse, we want you to know that there are resources available for you. We also want you to know that your case is particularly important to us.

While Matt was on active duty, he had the interesting responsibility of both prosecuting cases, as well as working with the Navy's Family Advocacy Program in their Case Review Committee process. We (Matt and Charlie) believe there are many, many wonderful social workers, clinicians, counselors, and chaplains that have chosen to work in this field and who are there to assist active duty servicemembers and their dependents. Most of the resources available to you are free of charge, and we particularly encourage you to search these resources out. Remember what we said in the beginning of the book - you need to take care of yourself first - and then worry about shielding your children and other loved ones in this process. Think about the wonderful folks at Family Advocacy as people who want to help you with your oxygen mask - and we promise you won't be disappointed.

It is important to note that all Family Advocacy Programs are set up under a Department of Defense Directive. All branches of service have a Family Advocacy Program. Once a report of domestic violence is made, a military commander can choose to send the servicemember to the Family Advocacy Program. The entire purpose of the program is to intervene and provide treatment - for the benefit of the entire family. In addition, there are counseling and support services, including group and individual services available to all dependents, including children.

Once a domestic abuse report is made to the Family Advocacy Program, a case worker is assigned to investigate and interview the victim and the accused to determine what steps, if any, should be taken. The victim is also assigned a Victim Advocate. Once the investigation is complete, the case is forwarded to the Case Review Committee - an independent panel of professionals from various disciplines (including medicine, law, mental health, social work, and a line commander) – all vote on whether or not the allegation should be substantiated or not. If the Committee votes to substantiate a case of domestic violence, and the servicemember is the offender, he or she can be mandated to undergo counseling and rehabilitative treatment. A servicemember who then fails to undergo this treatment can be administratively separated from the armed forces as a treatment failure.

Matt literally sat on hundreds of these cases through the Case Review Committee as the Legal Representative on the panel. Many of the cases reviewed were gut-wrenching. If you are the victim in a domestic abuse situation, we urge you to contact the Family Advocacy Program at the nearest military base for assistance.

It is also important to note that under the Uniformed Services Former Spouses' Protection Act, there is a specific provision that allows a spouse who is the victim of domestic abuse to receive his or her share of retired pay and benefits, even though the servicemember does not retire. This essentially means that it is possible you could receive a share of the now non-existent retired pay – however, you would need to qualify and meet several requirements. This is codified under 10 U.S.C. § 1408(h), and you must have a court order awarding you part of the servicemember's disposable retired pay as property. The servicemember must also have sufficient years of creditable service for retirement, and the servicemember must have lost the right to retire due to domestic violence involving a dependent family member. You must also be the actual victim of the abuse or the parent of a child who is the victim.

Transitional Compensation

Even in the event the servicemember is not retirement eligible, there is something known as Transitional Compensation, a program established by Congress under 10 U.S.C. § 1059. This program provides temporary assistance to spouses and family members when a servicemember is court-martialed or administratively separated from the service following the abuse of a spouse or family member. The compensation includes temporary financial support, housing benefits, and access to health care and base facilities. This compensation, if awarded, lasts a minimum of 12 months and up to a maximum of 36 months. The duration depends in part on how much time is left of the servicemember's obligated active duty service. If the obligated service is less than 36 months, the duration of the payments will be the greater of the unserved portion or 12 months.

In Closing

As you have noticed, the divorce process can be complicated and uncomfortable. It doesn't need to be harrowing though, if you approach it from a position of strength and knowledge. In so many ways, endings are beginnings, and resolving your case favorably will free up resources and provide comfortable terms so that you and your children can start anew free and unencumbered.

If there's one take away, you are now aware of the many resources available to you (see the full resource list at the end of the book). Even if you are not in an abusive relationship, there are many helpful and resourceful clinicians, counselors, and social workers at Navy Fleet and Family Service Centers, Army Soldiers Family Support Centers, Air Force Family Readiness Centers, and at the Coast Guard Integrated Support Command - among others available on Marine Corps bases and even at the smaller installations. We encourage you to seek support from these wonderful and caring people.

Even if you are not comfortable using a military service center for counseling, we recommend you speak to a counselor - especially if you have children. It can be empowering to discuss the divorce process with a counselor who can help you deal with the myriad of questions and issues that will arise with special regard to your well-being and that of your children.

We hope the local legal resources provided at the end of the book are helpful, and we invite you to attend a seminar we put on at different times of the month called What Women Need to Know about Divorce. The seminars are held on the second Saturday of every month from 8:30 a.m. to 12 noon and on the third Tuesday of every month at the Virginia Beach location only from 6:30 p.m. to 9:30 p.m.

There are three seminar locations: one in Virginia Beach, one in Chesapeake, and one in Newport News. The Virginia Beach seminars are held at Virginia Beach Friends Meeting House, 1537 Laskin Road, across from Hilltop east Shopping Center. The Chesapeake seminars are currently held at Extended Stay America Hotel, 809 Greenbrier Circle, near the Chesapeake Conference Center. The Newport News seminars are currently held at the Hilton Garden Inn, 180 Regal Way, off Victory Boulevard, near Regal Cinemas. We're proud that these seminars have helped many Virginia women gain information and strength as they have made vital decisions. Some who attend choose to share and participate; others prefer to sit back and listen. If you would like more information on these seminars, just call 757-456-1574 or visit www.MonthlyDivorceSeminars.com. Pre-registration discounts are available.

There are many, many good family law attorneys that specialize in divorce and who are decent and kind human beings. Please use the information in this book to ask the right questions of your prospective attorney to insure that he or she will most effectively represent your interests with skill and passion. Then, put on your own oxygen mask! And look out for what is best for you and your children.

4RESOURCES

"TAKE AS MUCH TIME TO PLAN YOUR DIVORCE AS YOU DID TO PLAN YOUR WEDDING."

Steps to Prepare for Divorce

1. Consult an attorney about your legal rights and attend the seminar What Women Need to Know about Divorce. The seminars are held on the second Saturday of every month at 8:30 a.m. to 12 noon and on the third Tuesday of every month at the Virginia Beach location only from 6:30 p.m. to 9:30 p.m. There are three seminar locations: one in Virginia Beach, one in Chesapeake, and one in Newport News. The Virginia Beach seminar is held at Virginia Beach Friends Meeting House, 1537 Laskin Road, across from Hilltop East Shopping Center. The Chesapeake seminar is held at the Extended Stay America Hotel, 809 Greenbrier Circle, near the Chesapeake Conference Center. The Newport News seminar is held at the Hilton Garden Inn, 180 Regal Way, off Victory Boulevard, near Regal Cinemas.

2. Write a narrative for your attorney, detailing the date you began living together, the date you married, your children's birth dates, previous separations, when various assets were acquired, and the separate property either of you brought into the marriage or inherited.

3. Gather information about what you own and owe. You'll need copies of financial statements, tax returns, retirement plan documents, brokerage statements and insurance policies.

4. Obtain detailed information on each retirement plan in which you and your husband have participated.

5. Decide which assets you would like to keep if you divorce and what you are willing to give up. Consult with your accountant about the tax consequences of various options, especially for keeping the house.

6. Get preliminary estimates of the value of the property you own and list the debts that you owe. Pay bills and credit cards from joint funds before separation, so you don't get stuck with them later.

7. Find out what is in the safe deposit box. Secure both keys, if possible.

8. Prepare a spending history for last year from your checkbooks so you can determine future needs and decide where to cut back if necessary.

9. Before you separate, use joint funds to repair your automobile and home, buy clothes for yourself and your children, and get needed dental work and medical checkups. If you wait until after separation, those expenses will be yours alone.

10. Set aside cash reserves to use in the first few months of separation. Transfer your share of joint funds to your separate bank account.

11. Apply for credit cards in your own name. If possible, obtain credit cards with check writing privileges.

12. After separation, close joint credit card accounts, get control of both cards issued on accounts, or notify creditors that you will no longer be responsible for your husband's charges on accounts.

13. Open a post office box that you can use for your mail before you separate and while you are in the process of divorce.

14. Begin a divorce notebook in which you list all problems with impending separation and divorce. Also list each step that you take in the divorce process, including a synopsis of all telephone calls and conferences with your attorney and accountant. Keep good notes.

15. Divorce is scary, but it will be less so if you figure out the worst that could happen and decide in advance how you will deal with it. Investigate community resources that are available to you.

16. Explore your career options. Use the crisis of divorce to catapult yourself into a more satisfying future.

17. Begin negotiation discussions with your husband, as calmly as possible. Find out what his hot buttons are and where he is willing to make concessions.

18. Attend family law court proceedings and talk to family and friends who have recently been through a divorce. Get a feel for the territory you will be crossing.

19. Find a good therapist or support group to help you through the months ahead. Divorce is too traumatic to go through it alone.

20. Take your time and don't rush matters. Planning for divorce is best done deliberately and slowly. This is your chance for a new beginning.

Special thanks to Ginita Wall, CPA, CFP of San Diego, California for allowing Charlie Hofheimer to develop the "Second Saturday" seminar on the east coast and for allowing him to use this "steps to prepare for divorce" since 1990.

FINANCIAL RECORDS WITH WHICH EVERY WOMAN SHOULD BE FAMILIAR

1. Net Worth Statement
2. Copies of all notes signed by yourself and your husband (Include 1st and 2nd mortgages)
3. Copies of any guarantees on behalf of others signed by you or your spouse
4. Tax returns for the last 3 years
5. Benefit statements of your employer and spouse's employer (pension plan, profit sharing, 401K, IRA, etc.)
6. Life insurance policies on you, your spouse and children
7. Short term disability policies on you and your spouse
8. Long term disability policies on you and your spouse
9. Homeowner's policy
10. Umbrella liability policy
11. Car insurance policies
12. Health insurance policies
13. Long term care insurance policies

14. Other insurance policies (Mortgage payment, credit life, AAA policy, cancer policy, etc.)

15. All bank account statements

16. All credit card statements

17. All brokerage statements

18. Any military benefits

19. Copy of credit history (obtain from retail merchants and any other applicable agencies)

20. Inventory of personal property (written and video)

21. Applicable employment contracts

22. Copies of buy sell agreements

23. Copies of Partnership Agreements

24. Inventory of lock box

25. Power of Attorney for you and your spouse

26. Medical Power of Attorney for Babysitters

27. Durable Medical Power of Attorney for you and your spouse

28. Wills

29. Living Wills

30. Copies of any Wills or Trusts of which you are the beneficiary

31. Trusts

32. Social Security Benefits Statement

33. Pre Nuptial Agreements

34. Separation Agreements

35. Lease Agreements

36. Real Estate Contracts

37. Mutual Fund statements

38. Annuity Statements

THE HIGH COST OF DIVORCE VS. THE IRS

- Legal fees and court costs for getting a divorce are generally personal and non-deductible; however, professional fees paid for tax advice or to obtain a taxable spousal support award will be deductible on your tax return in the year paid, under the provisions of Internal Revenue Code Sec. 212, since they are attributable to determination of taxes or the production of income.
- Legal fees spent to increase spousal support payments or collect arrearages are also deductible, under the same theory, but that deductibility doesn't extend to the paying spouse. His legal costs incurred while attempting to reduce support payments or to defend against a claim for greater support are not deductible by him.
- Legal fees are only deductible by the person who incurs them. Legal fees are never deductible where one spouse is ordered to pay the other spouse's legal fees, since a taxpayer is allowed a deduction only for the costs of advice to him or her, not for advice to the other party.
- Even the portion of your legal expenses that is not currently tax-deductible may become deductible when you sell assets you receive. A portion of your attorney fees can be allocated among the different assets that you receive in the settlement and will be added to the tax basis of each. You must be able to show that those fees were for time spent defending title to assets or obtaining them for you. For example, the cost of preparing and filing a deed to put title to a property in your name alone can be added to the tax basis of the property and deducted when the property is sold.
- In order to claim a deduction for legal expenses incurred in a divorce, the attorney must make a reasonable allocation of the legal expenses between deductible and non-deductible advice. The allocation may be in the form of an opinion letter from the attorney, based on reliable time records of services rendered. Any fees paid to a specialized professional, such as a tax attorney or CPA, for tax and investment advice will be fully deductible. The best evidence of deductible fees is a statement appearing directly on the attorney's bills regarding the portion attributable to tax advice, securing taxable support, and obtaining assets.
- The fees that are currently deductible, such as those for tax advice or those for securing income, can only be claimed if you itemize deductions on Schedule A of Form 1040. They are claimed as miscellaneous deductions and are subject to the 2% of adjusted gross income floor.
- The costs of personal advice, custody issues, counseling, or legal action in a divorce are not deductible. It may be difficult to separate the non-deductible personal costs of divorce from the deductible costs, but if the potential deduction is sizeable, the additional effort required to ferret out the tax-deductible portion will be worthwhile.

RESOURCE CONTACT LIST

ABUSE

Battered Women's Hotlines, Shelters, Support Groups, and Information

National Resource Center for Domestic Violence 800-537-2238

National Domestic Violence Hotline (24 hour) 800-799-7233

Family Violence & Sexual Assault Hotline of VA.................800-838-8238

Response Crises Hotline.......................................757-622-4300

Center for Sexual Assault Survivors 757-599-9848

Norfolk: YWCA (Women in Crisis Program, shelter, etc.)
Support Group - Call for dates & times........................757-625-5570

Union Mission Family Shelter 757-623-0642

Virginia Beach: Samaritan House
& Safe Harbor Center Support Group...........................757-631-0710

Judeo Christian Outreach Center 757-491-2846

Chesapeake/Portsmouth: Hershelter (Help and Emergency
Response Support Group - Call for dates & times..............757-485-3384

Suffolk: Genieve Shelter 800-969-4673

Hampton: Transitions Family Violence Services Support Group -
Call for dates & times 757-723-7774

Williamsburg: Avalon 757-258-5051

Gloucester: Laurel Shelter....................................804-694-5552

Victim/Witness Assistance Programs

Accomack County 757-787-8538

Chesapeake 757-382-6417

Gloucester County...757-693-1227

Hampton. 757-727-6442

Isle of Wight County 757-357-7403

Newport News 757-926-7443

Norfolk. 757-664-4850

Portsmouth 757-393-8729

Suffolk 757-923-2222

Virginia Beach 757-385-8301

York County / Poquoson 757-890-3402

Yorktown. 757-890-3401

Matthews 804-725-1291

Battered Women Support Groups

Chesapeake/Portsmouth Battered Women's
Support Group - Hershelter . . . . .757-485-3384 or 757-382-8172

Norfolk Battered Women's Support Group -
YWCA Women in Crisis Program. 757-625-4248

Hampton Transitions Family Violence Services 757-723-7774

Isle of Wight county Victim Witness Program Support Group . . .757-357-7403

Albemarle Hopeline, North Carolina. 252-338-3011

Virginia Beach Domestic Violence Police Unit
(M - F 8am - 12 midnight) 757- 385-4101

Pace (Police Assisted Community Enforcement)
Norfolk Social Services Department 757-664-6016

Child Abuse Information

Prevent Child Abuse Hampton Roads 757-440-2749

Virginia Child Abuse and Neglect Hotline -
VA Dept. of Social Services 800-552-7096

Prevent Child AbuseVirginia 800-244-5373

National Child Abuse Hotline - Child Help USA.................800-422-4453

Norfolk Child Abuse and Neglect (24 hour) -
Child Protective Services.......................................757-664-6022

FACTS (Families of Abused Children Traumatized Sexually) -
Vera Dammert..757-481-9521

DOMESTIC VIOLENCE ADVOCACY UNITS, COURT INTAKE AND CLERKS, MAGISTRATES

Accomack County

J & D Court Clerk 757-787-0920

Chesapeake

J & D Court
Intake......................................757-382-8150 or 757-382-8170

Clerk...757-382-8100

Magistrate 757-382-6632

Franklin City J & D Court Clerk 757-562-8559

James City County /Williamsburg J & D Court Clerk 757-564-2200

Hampton

J & D Court
Intake 757-727-6357

Clerk...757-727-6147

Magistrate 757-727-6589

Isle of Wight County

J & D Court Clerk 757-365-6237

Newport News

J & D Court
Intake..757-926-8781

Clerk...757-926-3603

Magistrate 757-926-8475

Norfolk

SAFE (Spousal Abuse Friend & Educator Program) 757-664-7647

Friends of the Norfolk Juvenile Court, Inc. 757-664-7649

J & D Court
Intake...757-664-7610

Clerk..757-664-7340

Magistrate 757-664-4799

Northampton County

J & D Court Clerk 757-678-0466

Portsmouth

FAIR (Friendly Advocates in Intimate Relationships) 757-397-2799

Friends of the Portsmouth Juvenile Court 757-397-2799

J & D Court
Intake...757-393-8571

Clerk..757-393-8851

Magistrate 757-393-8648

Southampton County J & D Court Clerk 757-653-2673

Suffolk

J & D Court...757-514-7790

Court Services Unit 757-514-4311

Magistrate 757-514-4301

Virginia Beach 2nd District Court Services Unit

FANS (Family Advocacy Network Services)..................... 757-385 -4361

J & D Court

Intake . . . . .757-385-4361 or 757-385-4362

Clerk 757-385-4391

Magistrate 757-385-4724

MILITARY RESOURCES

American Legion Family Support Network Hotline
(financial and family assistance) 800-504-4098

Ex-Pose (Ex-Partners of Servicemen [Women] for Equality) 703-941-5844

Fleet and Family Support Centers . . . . .www.ffscnorva.navy.mil

Naval Amphibious Base, Little Creek 757-462-7563

Naval Base, Norfolk 757-444-2102

Chesapeake, NW 757-421-8770

Naval Air Station, Oceana 757-433-2912

Naval Weapons Station, Yorktown 757-887-4606

Newport News Shipbuilding 757-688-6289

Dam Neck 757-492-7150

Norfolk Naval Shipyard 757-396-1255

Newport News 757-688-6289

New Parent Support Program Offices

Langley AFB . . . . .757-222-7130 ext. 3

Langley AFB Family Advocacy Program 757-764-2427

Navy Family Advocacy (addresses prevention, identification, treatment, follow-up & reporting child abuse, neglect & spouse abuse)

Naval Amphibious Base, Little Creek 757-462-7563

Family Advocacy Social Worker (After Hours) 757-953-5008

Naval Air Station, Oceana . . . . .757-433-2555 or 757-433-2558

Naval Base, Norfolk 757-444-2230

Naval Medical Center, Portsmouth 757-953-7801

Naval Weapons Station, Yorktown 757-887-4301

Naval Security Group Activity, NW - Chesapeake 757-421-8770

Navy Legal Assistance Offices

Naval Amphibious Base, Little Creek 757-462-4759

Naval Station, Norfolk . . . . .757-341-4489 or 757-341-4470

Naval Air Station, Oceana . . . . 757-433-2230 ext. 223

Naval Medical Center, Portsmouth 757-953-5452

Naval Legal Assistance Dept. - call for info . . .757-341-4489 or 757-341-4470
Website: www.ffscnorva.navy.mil
E-mail: navfamcenter@nwsy.navy.mil

www.militaryK12link.com (Hampton Roads school info - includes localities, transferal info, etc. - part of Fleet and Family Support)

Tri - Care (Military Medical HMO) 757-953-6708

Army: Soldiers & Family Support Center

Ft. Eustis 757-878-0901

Ft. Monroe 757-788-3878

Ft. Story 757-422-7311

Langley AFB Airmen & Family Readiness Center 757-764-3990

Langley AFB Family Advocacy 757-764-2427

Langley AFB Legal Assistance 757-764-3277

USCG EAP Program - Yorktown 757-856-2161

US Coast Guard Integrated Support Command -
Family Advocacy 757-686-4036

USCG MLCLANT (Legal Assistance) 757-628-4192

Navy - Marine Corps Relief Society (primarily for financial counseling)

Norfolk Office 757-423-8830

Little Creek Office 757-464-9364

Oceana Office 757-433-3383

Portsmouth Office...757-953-5956

COMMUNITY RESOURCES

Second Saturday - What Women Need to Know
About Divorce - Voice Mail Hotline 757-456-1574

United Way (Family, financial counseling & other extensive services)

Norfolk Understanding People Center.........................757-622-7017

Portsmouth 757-397-2121

Information and Referral Services of the Planning Council 757-625-4543

ODU Women's Center...757-683-4109

TCC Regional Women's Center ....www.tcc.edu/womenscenter

Portsmouth Campus..757-822-2160

Norfolk Campus 757-822-1140

Chesapeake Campus 757-822-5133

Virginia Beach Campus 757-822-7363

Virginia Wesleyan College....................................757-455-3200

Departments of Social Services

Chesapeake 757-382-2000

Hampton..757-727-1800

James City County...757-259-3100

Newport News (Denbeigh Office) 757-396-3160

Newport News (Jefferson Avenue Office) 757-926-6300

Norfolk. 757-664-6000

Portsmouth 757-405-1800

Suffolk 757-923-3000

Virginia Beach 757-437-3200

Williamsburg 757-220-6161

York County/Poquoson 757-890-8737

Virginia Department of Social Services (Eastern Region -
VA Beach Field Office) 757-491-3990

Division of Child Support Enforcement Pendleton
Child Service Center 757-437-2100

Community Services Board - City of Virginia Beach

Mental Health Emergency Services. 757-385-0888

Child and Youth Services

MESA Mutual Education Support & Advocacy 757-385-0802

MST In-Home Services 757-385-0834

Outpatient Child and Youth 757-437-6200

AFFORDABLE COUNSELING WHERE YOU LIVE

Community Services Board - City of Norfolk 757-441-5300

Community Services Board - City of Chesapeake. 757-547-9334

Community Services Board - City of Portsmouth. 757-393-8618

Community Services Board - City of Hampton/Newport News. .757-245-0217

Community Services Board - City of Virginia Beach. 757-437-3200

Community Services Board - City of Suffolk. 757-255-7100

Catholic Charities of Eastern VA - Virginia Beach
Access to Therapy (ACT PROGRAM) Sliding Fee Scale 757-467-7707

Catholic Charities of Eastern VA -
Chesapeake/Portsmouth (ACT) 757-484-0703

Catholic Charities of Eastern VA - Newport News (ACT)........757-875-0060

Catholic Charities of Eastern VA - Norfolk (ACT) 757-533-5217

Jewish Family Services of Tidewater 757-459-4640

United Methodist Family Services of Virginia...................757-490-9791

Hampton's Healthy Families Partnership.......................757-224-8450

DIVORCE/SEPARATION GROUPS

Divorce Care @King's Grant Baptist Church, Va Beach,
co -ed (call for dates and times) 757-340-0902

Divorce Care @Avalon Church of Christ, Va Beach, co-ed
(call for dates and times).....................................757-420-5208

Divorce Care @London Bridge Baptist Church, co-ed
(call for dates and times).....................................757-486-7900

Divorce Care @ Church of the Ascension (Catholic).............757-499-0843

Divorce Recovery Group @First Baptist Church of Norfolk,
co -ed, call for information 757-461-3226

Starting Over (Ministry for separated, divorced
or widowed individuals) 757-499-0843

PARENTING, COUPLES, CHILDREN'S RESOURCES

Barry Robinson Center -
A Behavioral Health System for Youth . . . . www.barryrobinson
757-455-6100 or 800-221-1995

Child Help USA 800-4ACHILD

Children in the Middle (support group for
children of divorcing parents - Jewish Family Services
of Tidewater) 757-459-4640

Compassionate Friends (Bereavement support group
for parents who have lost a child/children) 757-482-5856

YMCA Parenting Programs (Variety of parent support groups
plus classes for parents of younger children and teens) 757-622-9622

Parents Without Partners ....757-545-0386 or 757-498-2666

PAIRS (Intensive, comprehensive classes for couples skill
building & relationship work) contact Marc Rabinowitz 757-622-9852

PREP (Marriage Enrichment Program offered by YMCA
Parenting Programs 757-622-9622

Seton House (Runaway Teen Support, Shelter and Counseling)
24 hour hotline...............................757-498-HELP or 757-498-4357

Happily Parenting Teens (Seton House).........................757-306-1840

Grandparents as Parents Support Group - GAP
(Catholic Charities of Hampton Roads) 757-456-2366

Kids Cope - Catholic Family Services - for children 6 - 12;
dealing with divorce and separation 757-467-7707

Kids Priority One - kidspriorityone.org - excellent resource
for all things concerning family in the community 757-244-5373

www.militaryK12link.com - Hampton Roads school info, includes localities,
transferal info, etc., part of Navy Fleet and Family Support

Center for Child and Family Services,
2021 Cunningham Dr., Hampton, VA 757-838-1960

CHILD CARE AWARE PARENT NETWORK:.........www.ccaparentnetwork.org

Parenting Resources for Virginia Beach Email:........ VBparents@VBgov.com

Child Support Enforcement

STATE............................ www.dss.state.va.us/family/dcseoffices.cgi
800-481-1004
800-462-8386
800-828-1304

LEGAL RESOURCES
Approved Court mandated custody/parenting programs

And How Are the Children?
(Presented by Pendleton Child Service Center) 757-385-4537

Children and Divorce
(Presented by Navy Fleet and Family Support) . . . . .call any FFSC

Children First -
Chesapeake Volunteers in Youth Services . . . . .757-382-8184, intake

Cooperative Co-parenting Seminars
(presented by Mediation Center of Hampton Roads) 757-624-6666

Cooperative Co-parenting - Issues Surrounding
Separation and Divorce Catholic Charities of Eastern VA 757-467-7707

The UP Center Understanding People Program 757-622-7017

Legal Aid Society of Eastern Virginia

Hampton 757-275-0080

Norfolk 757-627-5423

Legal Services of Eastern Virginia (LSEVA)

Hampton 757-827-5078

Virginia Beach 757-552-0026

Williamsburg 757-220-6837

Eastern Shore (Bell Haven, VA) 757-442-3014

Lawyers Referral Service (Hampton Roads) 757-623-0132

Virginia Lawyer Referral Service 800-552-7977

Virginia Conflict Resolution Center (VCRC) -Mediation 757-480-2777

Mediation Center of Hampton Roads - Mediation 757-624-6666

Samaritan House 757-631-0710

Virginia Poverty Law Center 800-868-8752

Martindale-Hubbell Lawyer Locator at
Public Law Library or online at:........................... www.lawyers.com

Hofheimer/Ferrebee P.C., Representing Only Women in
Custody and Divorce - www.virginiadivorceattorney.com 757-425-5200

General legal information site -
find attorneys, legal information, etc......................www.lawinfo.com

Virginia Bar Association.. www.vba.org
....804-644-0041

Virginia State Bar Association .... www.vsb.org
....804-775-0500

Virginia Beach Bar Association ....www.vbbarassoc.com

Information on all Virginia courts, by type and by city .www.courts.state.va.us

Metropolitan Richmond Women's Bar Association ....www.mrwba.org

Debt Counseling Programs

Home Owners Hope Hotline 1-888-995-4673

United Way Affiliated Debt Counseling Programs

Stop Organization 757-858-1360

Catholic Charities of Eastern VA 757-484-0703

STAGES OF DIVORCE

It has been observed that divorcing persons move through a natural progression of stages of divorce. Every person experiences these stages differently. (Some may skip a stage or two). Since divorce adjustment has its roots in the marriage, that is where we will begin.

Stage 1: Disillusionment

Disillusionment begins when two spouses realize there are some very real differences between them. The person who is to fulfill almost all one's expectations, needs and ideals turns out to be depressed, sloppy, boring, unaffectionate, anti-social, uncaring, insensitive, etc., etc. While these thoughts and statements intrude on the happiest of marriages, prolonged time spent dwelling on them sows the seeds of destruction.

Stage 2: Erosion

The state is characterized by a chipping away of each other's egos. One or the other says "I'm not getting enough out of this marriage." Sometimes, a careful vigilance is maintained to make sure that one does not give any more than the other. The concentration in this period is on taking rather than giving, being loved instead of loving. Sex becomes a battleground where frigidity or impotency expresses the frozen anger.

Stage 3: Detachment

In the detachment stage the couple no longer cares enough to hate or fight. Each feels a low commitment to the relationship; they barely talk, avoid physical affection or sex, don't look into the others' eyes, etc.

This period is not so much one of an intensified conflict as it is increasing boredom with the conflict. The coldness that was at first withholding of love has become habitual and natural. Empty hulls of people pass each other in routine. The detached person begins to dream of his or her own future without the spouse.

Stage 4: Physical Separation

For those who have spent a long time preparing to get divorced by building up the courage to leave an intolerable marriage, the physical separation can bring enormous relief. For those who are unprepared and still emotionally involved in the spouse, physical separation can leave a person in shock. But most all newly separated persons have to face the loneliness, anxiety, initial confusion and fears.

The American culture nourishes insidious fears of loneliness. Being alone with one's self represents nothingness, a void to most people. We are learning that loneliness can also be creative. Out of loneliness comes strong determination, courage and deep commitment. Anxiety is another common emotion following physical separation–fear of the unknown. The future is uncertain. Many divorcing individuals change their vacations, lifestyles, residences and friends. The separated person may worry about meeting financial needs, about being attractive to the opposite sex, about the effect of divorce on children, etc., etc.

Separation brings new anxieties.

Stage 5: Mourning

Mourning is a web of anger, hurt, loneliness, relief and helplessness. Mourning helps rid one's self of the ghosts. A person says "I can't go back . . . but I can't go forward." They want intimacy but feel they can't handle it. In this stage, the divorcing person moves from no goals to concrete goals. They will take off the wedding ring, rearrange the furniture and "clean out the old house," and begin as a single person.

Mourning during divorce may unleash anger. Releasing anger is a necessary part of divorce. Depression may also accompany mourning.

Stage 6: Second Adolescence

Instead of looking back on the former spouse with anger and attraction the person during this stage is concentrating on his/her personal growth. Choices begin to increase. Vision clears. The excitement of possible new adventures and new risks creates an almost adolescent state. Previous areas of deprivation, whether sexual, travel, fun, hobbies, friends, or training are often vigorously pursued.

Dating often renews old adolescent feelings. "Is he/she going to call? Will he/she accept the invitation? Are my social skills ok according to today's standard?" A divorcing person may feel considerable intrigue and excitement during this stage.

Stage 7: Exploration and Hard Work

With renewed vitality, the divorcing individual begins earnestly to pursue self-chosen goals. Instead of seeing overwhelming, unreachable future aspirations, a plan of action toward manageable, reachable goals has been implemented. New relationships are formed, old ones with children are enhanced.

You may feel a new confidence, a sense of being master over your life.

Summary Chart of Former Spouse Benefits

Years of Marriage	Direct Pay from DFAS (if court awarded)	Survivor Benefit Plan – SBP* (if court awarded)	Military Medical Care**	Commissary	Exchange
20-20-20 Rule	Yes	Yes	Yes	Yes	Yes
20-20-15 Rule Divorced before 4/1/1985	Yes	Yes	Yes	No	No
20-20-15 Rule Divorced after 4/1/1985 but before 9/30/1988	Yes	Yes	The later of: a 2 Year Period or Until 12/31/1988	No	No
20-20-15 Rule Divorced after 9/30/1988	Yes	Yes	1 Year from Date of Divorce	No	No
10-10 Rule	Yes	Yes	No	No	No
Less than 10 Rule	No – Service member pays former spouse directly	Yes	No	No	No

* For conditions, refer to section on "Survivor Benefit Plan."
** Medical benefits are not granted if the former spouse is covered by an employer-sponsored health care plan. Refer to section on "Military Medical Care, Commissary and Exchange Privileges" for further information.

ABOUT THE AUTHORS

Matt Hamel joined Hofheimer Ferrebee, P.C., because, in a lot of ways, it reminded him of serving in the United States Navy. Hofheimer/Ferrebee, like the United States Navy, is dedicated to a mission that is larger than any one individual staff member. Each and every person in this firm is dedicated to the successful mission of guiding women through what is arguably the most difficult and emotionally traumatic time in her life.

Charlie Hofheimer has devoted much of his career protecting the interests of thousands of women contemplating or confronting divorce or contested custody cases. He is the co-founder of Hofheimer Ferrebee, P.C., along with his wife of 45 years and paralegal, Diane Hofheimer, and their daughter and attorney Kristen Hofheimer because they sensed a need to create a compassionate community of professionals to assist in educating and representing women as they navigate through the divorce process with a sense of confidence and a feeling of support. Today, Hofheimer Ferrebee is an 8-lawyer firm, 100 percent dedicated to representing only women in Family Law.

Since 1990, Charlie has conducted monthly three-hour seminars on "What Women Need to Know About Divorce." His seminar program, locally known as "Second Saturday" has been recognized by the Virginia State Bar for its outreach to the women of Virginia. Charlie has held numerous professional positions including Chairman of the Family Law Section of the Virginia Trial Lawyers Association for two successive terms, a founding member of the Virginia College of Trial Advocacy, a founding member and past chair of the Collaborative Divorce Solutions of Tidewater and Collaborative Divorce Solutions of the Virginia Peninsula, founding member and a past chair of Virginia Collaborative Professionals, a statewide organization promoting multi-disciplinary team collaborative divorce, and an emeritus member of the Hoffman I'Anson Inn of court. For the past three years, Charlie has been designated a Virginia Family Law "Super Lawyer" by superlawyer.com (a Thomson-Reuters Company) and holds the highest rating "10" available by www.avvo.com

Before joining Hofheimer/Ferrebee, Matt served for six years on active duty as a Navy JAG Attorney and he is still an active, drilling Navy JAG Reservist. Matt served his first two years on active duty in the Navy's busiest litigation office as a prosecutor and then volunteered for a tour of duty in Iraq during the "surge". He was stationed on board Forward Operating Base Camp Cropper in Baghdad, Iraq. He was attached to Task Force 134, which handled

Detainee Operations - and was responsible for the "parole-style" review boards of the highest value detainees to include the former Ba'athist Party members and "Deck of Cards" detainees. He then served the last few years of active military service as the Staff Judge Advocate to the Commodore, Destroyer Class Squadron and as the Assistant Force Judge Advocate to Commander, Naval Surface Force Atlantic Fleet. He also served on hundreds of Case Review Committees at Navy Fleet and Family Service Centers in Norfolk, Oceana, Little Creek, Northwest Annex and Yorktown. He was blessed with the opportunity to work with many wonderful social workers and licensed clinicians whose sole purpose is to assist military servicemembers and their dependents through very emotionally difficult, and oftentimes physically abusive relationships.

Matt knows what "divorce" feels like from a child's perspective...although he was an adult-child when this occurred. His parents were divorced after 33 years of marriage - and the divorce occurred even after he, as the adult-child, was married. This major family event was traumatic on him. This filled him with a sense of compassion and understanding for children who go through this process and also for the weaker party in a divorce case.

Representing women only in divorce and custody is much more than a job for Matt and Charlie. It is a passion. And, this book, <u>What Every Virginia Military Wife Needs to Know About Divorce</u>, is much more than a book. It is our way to pay homage to military wives and female service members who serve our great country.